GREAT SOURCE

# WriteTraits

## Student Traitbook

Vicki Spandel and Jeff Hicks

# GREAT SOURCE®

HOUGHTON MIFFLIN HARCOURT

www.greatsource.com
800-289-4490

## Acknowledgements

For permission to reprint copyrighted material, grateful acknowledgement is made to the following sources:

Excerpt from *A Natural History of the Senses* by Diane Ackerman. Text copyright © 1990 by Diane Ackerman. Reprinted by permission of Random House, Inc.

Excerpt from *The Animal Dialogues: Uncommon Encounters in the Wild* by Craig Childs. Published by Little, Brown and Company. Text copyright © 1997, 2007 by Craig Childs. Reprinted by permission of Hachette Book Group, Inc.

Excerpt from *Bull Run* by Paul Fleischman. Text copyright © 1993 by Paul Fleischman. Reprinted by permission of HarperCollins Publishers and Paul Fleischman.

Excerpt from *Dave at Night* by Gail Carson Levine. Text copyright ©1999 by Gail Carson Levine. Reprinted by permission of HarperCollins Publishers.

Excerpt from *Escape! The Story of the Great Houdini* by Sid Fleischman. Text copyright © 2006 by Sid Fleischman. Reprinted by permission of HarperCollins Publishers.

Excerpt from *Esperanza Rising* by Pam Muñoz Ryan. Published by Scholastic Press, a division of Scholastic Inc. Text copyright © 2000 by Pam Muñoz Ryan. Reprinted by permission.

Excerpt from *Heads or Tails: Stories from the Sixth Grade* by Jack Gantos. Text copyright © 1994 by Jack Gantos. Reprinted by permission of Farrar, Straus and Giroux, LLC.

Excerpt from *Lives of the Artists: Masterpieces, Messes (and What the Neighbors Thought)* by Kathleen Krull. Text copyright © 1995 by Kathleen Krull. Reprinted by permission of Houghton Mifflin Harcourt Publishing Company and Writer's House, LLC., on behalf of the author.

Excerpt from *Notes From a Liar and Her Dog* by Gennifer Choldenko. Text © 2001 by Gennifer Choldenko. Reprinted by permission of G.P. Putnam's Sons, a division of Penguin Young Readers Group, a member of Penguin Group (USA) Inc. and Curtis Brown Ltd., on behalf of the author.

Excerpt from *Saving Sweetness* by Diane Stanley. Text copyright © 1996 by Diane Stanley. Reprinted by permission of G. P. Putnam's Sons, a division of Penguin Young Readers Group, a member of Penguin Group (USA) Inc.

Excerpt from *Voyage of a Summer Sun: Canoeing the Columbia River* by Robin Cody. Text copyright © 1995 by Robin Cody. Reprinted by permission of Alfred A. Knopf, Inc, a division of Random House, Inc.

ISBN-13  978-0-669-01516-4

ISBN-10  0-669-01516-4

1 2 3 4 5 6 7 8 9 10   1409   18 17 16 15 14 13 12 11 10

4500237787

# About the Authors

## Jeff Hicks

Jeff taught for 18 years in the Beaverton School District (home of the 6-traits) where he enjoyed working with students to help them find their voices as writers. He is the co-author of *Write Traits Classroom Kits*, *Write Traits Advanced*, and *Write Traits Kindergarten*. Though his heart is still in the classroom, he is now a full-time writer, presenter, and professional development consultant. He lives in Beaverton with his wife and son, and he currently serves on the Beaverton School Board.

## Vicki Spandel

Vicki is a founding coordinator of the 17-member teacher team that developed the original, nationally recognized 6-trait model for writing assessment and instruction. A specialist in teaching writing and revision to students of all ages, she is the author of *Write Traits Classroom Kits*, *Write Traits Advanced*, and *Write Traits Kindergarten*, as well as *The 9 Rights of Every Writer*, *Creating Writers*, and *Creating Young Writers*. She makes her home in the town of Sisters, Oregon, bordering the beautiful Three Sisters Wilderness.

# Contents

# UNIT 4: WORD CHOICE

# UNIT 5: SENTENCE FLUENCY

# UNIT 1

# Ideas

As a seasoned writer, you know that successful writing begins and ends with clear, compelling ideas. Of course, ideas may not seem all that intriguing—at first. Picture some plain cookie dough sitting on a kitchen counter somewhere, awaiting a chef's magic touch. That dough has potential, certainly. It could turn into something mouthwatering, but that would take work—the addition of chips, nuts, or perhaps some delectable flavorings. Then the raw dough would need to be shaped, cut, and baked. Finally, fresh-from-the-oven cookies could be arranged on a plate and presented to eager guests. In a sense, first-writing thoughts are a little like raw cookie dough. They must be worked and shaped before they're ready to be consumed by hungry readers.

**In this unit, you'll practice planning and shaping Ideas so that the results are positively enticing. You'll learn to**

- prewrite by drawing or listing details.
- narrow your topic to make it manageable.
- give vague writing focus and clarity.
- use feedback to revise writing so that it holds a reader's attention.

## Sample Paper 1
## Score for Ideas _____

# A Special Moment

This year my family took a vacation to Hawaii. It was so cool! In case you do not know, Hawaii is this really long chain of islands in the Pacific Ocean. They are very green and beautiful. The ocean is a beautiful blue color. There is a lot to do in Hawaii, such as shopping or swimming or taking pictures of the beautiful scenery. Or you can just walk on the beach and watch the sunset. It is so beautiful! The colors are amazing! You see all these different shades of blue. While we were in Hawaii, my Aunt Beth went swimming with the dolphins. You have to go to a special place to do this. One of the dolphins was named Dolly. She was very friendly. We have a picture of them together, and it is so cool. That was a special moment. If you get a chance to go to Hawaii, be sure you do it! It takes a while to get there. (Well, that depends on where you live, of course!) You will not forget it! It is a beautiful place.

## Sample Paper 2
## Score for Ideas _____

# Boomer

I thought I'd be 40 years old before I would get my first dog. I had been dropping hints and flat out begging to get a dog for months. Then one day my Mom picked me up from school and whisked me off to a farm where golden retriever puppies were for sale. We left with a great puppy that we named Boomer. The name fit perfectly.

From day one, he just boomed through the house. Boom! Into the couch. Boom! Into the cupboards. Boom! Into the bedroom door. We loved Boomer, but it wasn't easy. He chewed on everything, including my dad's watchband, the newspaper, tablecloths and bedspreads, laundry, the carpet, and lamp cords. It seemed like everything we owned was either damp or full of holes.

Puppies leave other messes, too. Boomer didn't get the part about going outside before "doing his business," as Mom called it, so I had some unpleasant work to do cleaning the kitchen floor, the bathroom floor, and the living room carpet! After a month of messes and stains, Boomer was finally trained, but by then, we needed new carpeting.

If I had known how much trouble Boomer would be, I would probably have left him at the kennel. That would have been a huge mistake. Boomer sleeps by my bed, forgives my bad moods, puts up with cold baths or getting stuffed into the crowded back seat of a small car, listens patiently to every story like it's the best thing he ever heard, keeps me company on walks no matter what the weather is like, takes my side in every debate (I can tell by his expression), and is always up for a game of Frisbee, day or night. You can't ask for more from any friend.

# Ideas

**The WRITER...**
makes everything crystal clear, beginning to end.

**So the READER...**
_____
_____
_____

**The WRITER...**
keeps the message small and focused.

**So the READER...**
_____
_____
_____

**The WRITER...**
chooses details with care.

**So the READER...**
_____
_____
_____

**The WRITER...**
knows the topic inside and out.

**So the READER...**
_____
_____
_____

# Think, See, Draw!

**W**riters do a lot of things to warm up, or *prewrite.* Some discuss their ideas with friends—who may raise important questions or come up with details that the writer didn't think of. Many writers make lists or webs to help them see the connections between the smaller parts of a big idea. And others draw.

Now, you may or may not think of yourself as an artist, but either way, drawing can help you extend your thinking. That's because the very *act* of drawing helps pull out details you didn't even know were in your head. What's more, a sketch records your idea in a physical way, giving you something to look at as you write. Drawing is a way of coaching yourself.

## First Thoughts

Prewriting can help you take an oversized topic and make it both smaller and—even more important—personal to *you.* Let's try an example. Consider this big topic: "Fun in the Great Outdoors." What pops into your head when you think of this topic?

Write down some first thoughts here—just key words or phrases—as quickly as they come to you:

1. _____

2. _____

3. _____

4. _____

# Ideas

## A Question

Do you think everyone in your class is thinking and writing the same things?

☐ Yes, absolutely.

☐ No, that's pretty unlikely.

## Another Question

Look carefully at this list of outdoor activities:

- Boating
- Hiking
- Rafting
- Fishing
- Rock climbing
- Skateboarding
- Camping

On a scale of 1 (low) to 10 (high), how helpful is this list in making you feel ready to write?

| 1 | 2 | 3 | 4 | 5 | 6 | 7 | 8 | 9 | 10 |

Not one bit helpful!

*Really* helpful!

Do you feel ready to write about this topic without any further thought?

☐ Yes, I'm ready! Somebody get me a pencil—quick!!

☐ No, but I could do it with effort.

☐ No! I don't have one clue what I would say first.

If you said yes, good for you! If you said no, we're going to show you a strategy that may help when first thoughts (or suggestions) are not enough.

# Picture It—Then, Draw It

Look back at your answer to the question, *What pops into your head when you think of the topic "Fun in the Great Outdoors"?* Maybe your first thoughts were connected to an outdoor activity on our list—or maybe not. Use scratch paper to draw a quick and simple sketch of what "fun in the great outdoors" means to you. Spend about 5–6 minutes sketching. (Don't worry about your artistic skills—this drawing is for you to use *as a writer*. It's not going to hang in the Guggenheim Museum.)

## Review and Reflect

Take a minute to reflect on your sketch by asking yourself these questions:

- Are you in the picture? Is anyone else?
- What, specifically, are you doing?
- Why did you focus on *this* particular moment or event?
- Does this picture help you recall good memories?
- Which details are *most important?* (Did you forget anything?)
- What just happened—or is about to happen?

Give your picture a title that reflects the main idea—or reflects what is most important to you. Examples:

- *First Fish*
- *Central Park in Winter*
- *Camping Memories*
- *Championship Game*

Title of my sketch: _____

What have you done so far? Let's see . . . you've:

- ☐ drawn a sketch to 1) make a topic personal and 2) help you recall details.
- ☐ reflected on your drawing to recall even more.
- ☐ given your drawing a title that sums up the big idea.

You're *almost* ready to write. Here's one more important step—thinking about supporting details. For this, we'll use a connected, but slightly different, prewriting strategy.

## Brick by Brick

Think of details as the *bricks* you need to build a solid idea for readers. Inside each brick, include one detail that tells something important about your main idea. Look back at your sketch to help you come up with the details you need. Try to fill all six bricks—and add more if you need them.

### Build It for Your Readers

Now it's time to use those detail bricks to build a piece of writing. Think like a reader for a moment: Which brick holds the most *interesting* or *important* detail? That brick might be the best place to start.

On a separate sheet of paper, turn the words in your brick details into sentences that help create images, or pictures in your readers' minds. Write for 10 minutes or more. Remember that you can

- look back at your sketch for more ideas.
- add new details as you think of them.
- change your mind and leave out details you do not need.

## Share and Compare

Share your prewriting and writing with a partner. Listen carefully for specific details. Share your response to your partner's writing:

My partner's topic was completely different from mine.　　Yes ☐　　No ☐

The details in my partner's writing made a picture in my mind.　　Yes ☐　　No ☐

The picture in my mind was like the sketch my partner drew.　　Yes ☐　　No ☐

If not, how was it different? _____

_____

As my partner was reading, I thought of more questions I hoped the writing would answer.　　Yes ☐　　No ☐

If so, share those questions.

### A Writer's Question
Sketching helps a lot of writers get started—even if they're not very artistic. Why is the *act of drawing* more important than creating a work of art?

### Putting It to the Test
Let's say you are taking a writing test and you only have 30 minutes to write on a topic you have not seen before. Could it be a good use of your time to take 5 of those minutes to draw a quick sketch? Why or why not?

# narrowing Your Topic

**Y**ou're having one of those days . . . You only have one clean sheet of paper left. Your arm feels as heavy as lead. Your pen is almost out of ink and you can't find another and now your teacher wants you to write *everything you know* about one of these topics:

- Sports
- History of the World
- Living Things
- The Universe *(Oh, no. . . !)*

Hey! *Hey!!* **HEY, wake UP!!!!**

Whew. You're only dreaming. Lucky thing, too, because if you are like most writers, you know that topics like these are *waaay* too big and broad to tackle. The surprising thing is, though, that many young writers assign themselves big topics just like these—*even when they have a choice*. That's like trying to find a street in Riverton, Wyoming, by viewing Earth from outer space. Why make it so difficult when there's a simple solution? Come with us . . .

# Listening to Your Inner Navigator

Perhaps you have used a GPS (Global Positioning System) at some time to find your way to a new site—or to navigate an unfamiliar road. A GPS pinpoints your location and guides you, using visuals and aural directions, to your destination.

As a writer, you can narrow a big topic down to size by activating your *inner navigator* or **TPS**—**T**opic **P**inpointing **S**ystem. (Really, your TPS is nothing more than your writing brain on high power.) To activate your TPS, ask yourself questions that start with words like *who, what, when, where, why,* or *how.* Your answers will whittle a big, sprawling topic down to manageable size. Here's an example.

## TPS in Action

Big, Overwhelming, Vast, and Sprawly Topic: Sports

1. Inner Navigator: **What** do you want to say about sports?

2. Writer's Answer: I want to talk about an outdoor sport I love.

3. New Topic: Lacrosse (Smaller, but still too big for comfort.)


1. Inner Navigator: **What** do you like about lacrosse?

2. Writer's Answer: I like the action, equipment, and *history!*

3. New Topic: History of Lacrosse (Close, but we need an angle.)


1. Inner Navigator: **Why** is the sport's history so interesting?

2. Writer's Answer: Lacrosse was first played by Native Americans—but it has changed.

3. New topic: Native American Roots of Lacrosse (Ah—now we're getting somewhere!)

1. Inner Navigator: **How** will you show the ways it has changed?

2. Writer's Answer: I will compare modern Lacrosse to the earlier version.

3. Final topic: <u>Native American Lacrosse versus Today's Game</u> (Finally! Under control!)

## You're the Navigator

Where do those "inner navigator" questions come from? From YOU. So . . . it's time to activate your own TPS and see if you can narrow one of our topics down to size. (Later, you'll work on one of your own.)

This time around, work alone. You can then compare your final topic with the one your partner chooses. Good writers tend to be independent thinkers, so don't be surprised if your final topics are completely different!

Start with this Big Topic: <u>Animals</u>

Remember to
  • ask yourself questions. (Put your TPS to work!)
  • make your topic smaller and smaller, one step at a time.
  • make the topic personal—aim for a small topic YOU know and like.
  • use key words to help you think of helpful questions: *who, what, when, where, how,* and *why.*

Big Topic: <u>Animals</u>

1. Inner Navigator Question: _____

2. Writer's Answer: _____

3. New topic: _____


1. Question: _____

2. New topic: _____

**1.** Question: _____

**2.** New topic: _____


**1.** Question: _____

**2.** New topic: _____


**1.** One Last Question: _____

**2.** Final topic: _____

Do you like your final topic? If not, narrow it further.
YOU are the navigator!

## Share and Compare

Compare your final topic with the one your partner came
up with. Did you go in different directions? Which of the
following is true?

☐ Our final topics are just about identical!

☐ Our topics are different—mostly because one topic
is still way too big!

☐ Our topics are different, but both of us would be
ready to write.

# Charting Your Own Waters

This time, begin with a BIG topic of your own. Here are a
few ideas—but, by all means, choose any topic you like:

- Politics
- Food
- Technology
- Entertainment

Remember, ask as many questions as you need in order to
narrow your topic and feel *ready* to write. (That feeling of
readiness is how you know your topic is small enough.)
**Hint:** It may only take two or three questions to narrow
some topics and five or six questions to narrow others.

Name _____  Date _____

**My Original Oversized Topic:** _____

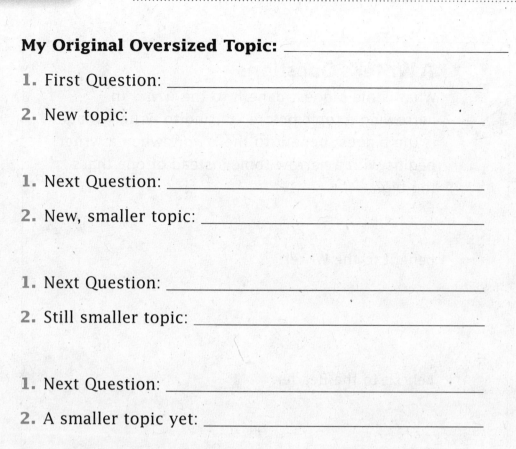

1. First Question: _____

2. New topic: _____

1. Next Question: _____

2. New, smaller topic: _____

1. Next Question: _____

2. Still smaller topic: _____

1. Next Question: _____

2. A smaller topic yet: _____

1. One Last Question: _____

2. Final oh-so-manageable topic: _____

Do you like your final topic? If not, narrow it further—or begin again. Don't write a single word until YOU, the navigator, are satisfied.

## Share and Compare

Compare your final topic with your partner's. Is either topic still too big? If so, help your partner (or let your partner help you) make that topic smaller.

When both topics are small enough (*Hey—how will you know that again?*), write for 10 minutes or more, using your own paper.

# Ideas

## A Writer's Questions

What is the biggest benefit to the *writer* in narrowing a topic before starting to write? What is the biggest benefit to the *reader* when a writer begins with a narrow topic instead of one that's too big?

Benefit to the Writer:

Benefit to the Reader:

## Putting It to the Test

You are taking a writing test and the topic feels really big. It might be one of these:

• Describe a day you'll never forget.

• Describe a person who has influenced you.

How could you use the strategies from this lesson to make that topic a little smaller and easier to manage when writing time is short?

# From Fuzzy to Focused

Your friend's family needs your help. They ask you to help move the whosiwhatsit over to the whatchacallit. If you're a *very* good sport, you might say yes without blinking. But if you're like most people, you might want to ask a question or two before you commit. Maybe your friend is moving his piano to a different room—up the stairs. Or, he is relocating his pet crocodile to the pond in your backyard. Hmm. Details do make a difference!

As a writer, you can leave your readers scratching their heads if you use fuzzy language and leave out important details. Not to worry! With a little practice, you can transform whosiwhatsit language into focused writing.

## Sharing an Example: *Esperanza Rising*

Carefully read this passage from Pam Muñoz Ryan's book *Esperanza Rising*. As you read, think about which details help form a clear picture in your mind.

Papa handed Esperanza the knife. The short blade curved like a scythe, its fat wooden handle fitting snugly in her palm. This job was usually reserved for the eldest son of a wealthy rancher, but since Esperanza was an only child and Papa's pride and glory, she was always given the honor. Last night she had watched Papa sharpen the knife back and forth across a stone, so she knew the tool was edged like a razor.

"*Cuídate los dedos,*" said Papa. "Watch your fingers."

Name _____  Date _____

. . . The clusters were heavy on the vine and ready to deliver. Esperanza's parents, Ramona and Sixto Ortega, stood nearby. Mama, tall and elegant, her hair in the usual braided wreath that crowned her head, and Papa, barely taller than Mama, his graying mustache twisted up at the sides. He swept his hand toward the grapevines, signaling Esperanza. When she walked toward the arbors and glanced back at her parents, they both smiled and nodded, encouraging her forward. When she reached the vines, she separated the leaves and carefully grasped a thick stem. She put the knife to it, and with a quick swipe, the heavy cluster of grapes dropped into her waiting hand. Esperanza walked back to Papa and handed him the fruit. Papa kissed it and held it up for all to see.

"*¡La cosecha!*" said Papa. "Harvest!"

*Esperanza Rising,*
by Pam Muñoz Ryan

## Your Mind's Eye—What Can You See?

Author Pam Muñoz Ryan carefully selected words and details that would invite readers inside her story. Though you may still have questions, the author has already shared many details about various characters and events. What *specific* details did this writer use to paint pictures in our minds? Work with a partner to complete the chart on the following page.

Name _____    Date _____

| Person, Place, Thing, or Event | Details that Make Clear Pictures |
|---|---|
| knife | *short blade ...* |
| Mama | |
| Papa | |
| grapes | |
| importance of cutting grapes | |

## Share and Compare

Share your chart with other classmates. As you see and hear what others wrote, feel free to add any details you may have missed.

## What if . . .

What if Pam Muñoz Ryan had written this very basic version of the passage above?

Her father handed her the knife. She cut the grapes and handed them to him.

Think like a *reader*. What is missing from this what-if version? Write down as many things as you can think of in two minutes. Then talk with a partner to expand your list.

1. _____
2. _____
3. _____
4. _____
5. _____
6. _____

## From Fuzzy to Focused (in a Lightning Flash)

The piece of writing called "A Bad Day" needs your help.
Follow these steps:

**1.** Read it carefully.

**2.** Close your eyes and try to picture what the author is writing about.

**3.** Read it again with a pencil in your hand.

**4.** Underline any fuzzy words or phrases. (Mark the margin with a lightning bolt.)

**5.** Revise the writing by adding sharper description and more precise words. **Hint:** As you revise, think like a reader. Hit those fuzzy lines with bolts of lightning. Write what you would like to read.

### Fuzzy Writing: "A Bad Day"

His car broke down on the road. The weather was bad, and

he would have to walk. It was far. He was going to be late for

work, and his boss would be mad. He felt pretty bad.

# Ideas

## Share and Compare

Share your writing with a partner or in a writing circle.
Check the things you or another writer did to make the
writing stronger:

☐ Changed words to make the meaning more clear

☐ Changed words to say things in a stronger or more
interesting way

☐ Added sensory details (sights, sounds, smells, feelings)

☐ Added dialogue

☐ Added strong verbs

Other changes: _____

Jot down some favorite words and phrases on a separate
piece of paper and be prepared to share these in your class
discussion.

### A Writer's Questions

Do you know anyone who writes like the what-if
version of the Pam Muñoz Ryan book? How does
that kind of detail-free writing affect most readers?
How does it affect you as a reader? Would you keep
reading a book that began in this way? Why?

### Putting It to the Test

You're writing a story or essay in a testing
situation, and you feel rushed. You settle for the
what-if version of things instead of including
details. How much, on a 6-point scale, do you think
that omission will affect your score? Do you think
you could raise your score by, say, a point just by
adding one or two significant, memorable details?
Why do small changes make a big difference?

# From Reader to Writer

In your classroom, you get to share your writing with classmates; taking turns reading, listening, and giving feedback. Readers don't always get to communicate directly with authors, though. Sometimes the writer isn't a member of your class. When you are reading library books, magazines, on-line articles, or blogs, does your brain come up with comments, questions, or suggestions? Maybe you want to say, "Tell me more!" Or, you have a polite complaint, "No fair stopping now! It was just getting interesting!" As a reader, you want certain things from writers: ideas that get your imagination churning, characters who seem as real as people next door, and answers to your most pressing questions. As a writer, make sure you provide those same things for *your* readers.

## "Dear Writer"

Read the following two examples. As a reader, do you have any unanswered questions? Does the writer need to give you *more* information—or do something *differently?* Use the space below each example to send a message to the writer.

# Ideas

**Hint:** Stay positive and *be specific*—writers have feelings, you know!

**Example 1**

## The Secret Woods

The last time we were at the beach, my friend and I hiked along a trail we always take. Suddenly, though, where we usually go left, for some reason we headed right. To the left were awesome, rolling sand dunes; to the right was the great unknown—at least unknown to us. The trail followed the ridge of a sandy hill, then cut sharply down to a thick, dark grove of trees. All along the trail were some animal tracks. Some seemed very fresh. We hesitated at the edge of the trees and then followed the tracks into the woods. In seconds, it got eerily quiet. We couldn't hear the ocean anymore. That sure was one great adventure!

*Dear Writer,*

_____

_____

_____

_____

_____

_____

_____

_____

_____

Example 2

## The Stray

I live in a tall apartment building in a big city. The elevator ride usually leaves my stomach feeling wobbly. We're on the 12th floor. The sign clearly says "No Pets," but people do have pets. They sneak them in. Mrs. Harwood on 7 has a pet, and Mr. Spiven on 11 has one, too. I know for sure that one person has a really *unusual* pet! So when I saw this forlorn stray in the alley, what was I supposed to do? Leave him to starve? I'm so glad I made the right decision. My life is so interesting now!

Dear Writer,

_____

_____

_____

_____

_____

_____

_____

_____

_____

## Message Received

*First* . . . in writing circles or as a class, share several of your Dear Writer letters aloud. List some of the best suggestions and comments.

*Next . . .* imagine you are one of the two writers receiving letters from readers. How would that influence your revision? Choose one piece to revise. Follow your own advice and that of your classmates. Take 10 minutes or more to write your revision on your own paper. Feel free to change information, add new details, or both. As you revise, keep asking yourself:

- Am I offering readers details that will keep them reading?
- Am I creating clear pictures in my readers' minds?
- Am I answering my readers' most important questions?
- Am I writing something I would like to read myself?

## Share and Compare

Share your revised writing with a partner. Listen carefully to the changes your partner made. Did his or her revision answer your questions? Did it make you want to read even more? Write down one question you still have on an index card, fold it, and hand it to your partner. (No peeking until all sharing is over.)

### A Writer's Questions

Good writers are always answering readers' questions. But . . . do they also raise new questions as they write? Is this a good thing? Why?

### Putting It to the Test

Let's say you're writing a story or essay in a testing situation. You have your topic clearly in mind, but you want to think like a reader. (After all, readers are going to score your work!) Do you think it could help to quickly jot down two or three questions your reader might have? If you did this and made sure to answer the questions, would it affect your score in the trait of Ideas? Why?

# Conventions & Presentation

**The WRITER...**
edits everything thoroughly.

**So the READER...**
_____
_____
_____

**So the READER...**
_____
_____
_____

**The WRITER...**
looks _and_ listens for errors.

**So the READER...**
_____
_____
_____

**The WRITER...**
uses conventions to bring out meaning and voice.

**So the READER...**
_____
_____
_____

**The WRITER...**
is thoughtful about presentation.

## Conventions and Presentation
## Editing Level 1: Conventions

# In Your Pocket

**Y**ou want your ideas, not your mistakes, to catch your reader's eye. How can you be sure that will happen? First you want some conventions—capitals at the start of a sentence, correct punctuation at the end, spelling of commonly-used words, basic grammar—to be in your pocket. In other words, you want to know some conventions so well that you take care of them automatically. Second you need to carefully edit everything you write by reading both silently and aloud, pencil in hand. Yes, it takes time and effort, but it's worth it. You know how you feel when you have to tidy up after someone else? That's how readers feel when they have to edit in their heads because the writer forgot to tidy up the text.

## A Warm-Up

What conventional skills do you have in your pocket? Or to put it another way, what are your strengths in the trait of Conventions? Think about

- Spelling
- Punctuation
- Grammar
- Paragraphing
- Capitalization

Reflect for a moment, then write your strengths on the numbered list below. Include up to five, focusing on the things you do BEST.

**In my pocket:**

1. _____

2. _____

3. _____

**4.** _____

**5.** _____

Now, let's turn the tables. What elements of Conventions are *not in your pocket*? What kinds of errors, if you are honest with yourself, do you frequently make in your own writing? List *up to five*—and if it helps, pull a sample of writing from your folder and look it over.

**Definitely NOT in my pocket:**

    **1.** _____

    **2.** _____

    **3.** _____

    **4.** _____

    **5.** _____

One more question: What kinds of errors bug you as a reader? What mistakes are you most likely to notice when you read a book, email, letter, ticker on television—even a grocery marquee? Again, list up to five, focusing on errors that annoy you most.

**Things that bug me as a reader:**

    **1.** _____

    **2.** _____

    **3.** _____

    **4.** _____

    **5.** _____

## Share and Compare

Compare your lists with a partner's list. Your lists will probably look different because they are personalized. However, look for similarities, too. Put an **X** next to the error you find *most annoying* as a reader. Put a double **XX** next to the error you struggle most with in your own writing.

# Breaking Down Barriers

The more you practice editing, the more conventional skills you'll have in your pocket to break down barriers that keep readers from focusing on your message. Read the following sample of writing carefully. How many conventional skills does this writer have in her pocket? How much editing do you have to do as a reader?

About a year ago, a New High School was built in neighborhood. It's within walking distance of my house, which is good for me. The problem is all the the extra traffic that now comes though our neighborhood.

There are a lot more cars than their used to be, and most of them are driven by younger drivers. This makes my parents very nervous. It seems as if there are more cars going to fast and fewer cars actually stopping at the intersection near our house. "Mina, my father said to me last night, "you've got to be extra careful crossing the street and riding your bike. "Trust me," I tells him, I want to live to be a seventh grader." The neighbors got together at the high School for a meeting with people from the city the police department and the school.

They came up up with a plain to put in speed bumps to slow down the. Now, all we has to do is get everone in the neighborhood to agree to the plan

## "Tidying Up" the Text

Now read the piece again as an editor, pencil in hand. We recommend that you

- read aloud, slowly, so you do not miss anything.
- have a handbook or other resources handy so you can check things out.
- use the correct marks from the copyeditor's poster.
- go back for one more look to be sure you didn't miss anything.

Take 5–6 minutes to edit this piece, and record the number of errors you find.

I found _____ errors.

## Share and Compare

Compare your editing with a partner's. Did you find the same errors—and the same number of errors? Did this writer by chance make mistakes that are problems for you, too? If your partner found something you missed or used a copyeditor's symbol you had forgotten, mark those changes on your paper, too. Then coach your teacher as he or she models the editing of this passage.

### A Writer's Questions

As an editor, you look for errors and correct them. As a *reviser*, your mission is a little different—you want to clarify or expand ideas, perhaps strengthen organization or voice. Look back at the passage you just edited. If you were to *revise* it, what are the top three things you would do? Talk with a partner about this and make a list. Be ready to share it with the whole class.

# Reaching the Audience

**W**hat if your writing were going to be

- displayed on a hallway bulletin board for students or guests to read?
- included in a school newspaper?
- sent home to parents in an informational flier?

When your writing is going to be published in some way, you need to think carefully about how it is presented to your audience. Presentation (Level 2 editing) ensures that your work is

- a good blend of text and art (photos, drawings, graphics).
- eye–catching enough to grab someone's attention.
- easy to scan for needed information.

Editing and presentation work together to make sure that readers can breeze right through your writing with no errors to distract them—and that they will notice, understand, and remember your message.

## Warm-Up

With your teacher's help, your class has gathered a collection of published materials. Look through them, focusing on presentation: general layout, use of blank space, pictures, art, and font types.

Don't spend too much time on any one piece. Try to see as many as you can. With a partner or in a writing circle, make two stacks: those pieces that are dramatic, eye catching, and effective—and those you'd be less likely to notice or give attention. Then brainstorm at least five or six standout features you think are important in good presentation.

**Important Presentation Features:**

1. _____

2. _____

3. _____

4. _____

5. _____

6. _____

# Presentation Practice

### "Must-See" (or "Must-Miss") TV

Following are two printed advertisements for new television reality shows designed for young people ages 11 to 17. (The television programs they advertise are NOT real.) Each one is trying to excite potential viewers.

Does one catch your eye more than the other? Is there one that says "Notice me! This is for you! Program the DVR!"? With your partner, look over your list of important presentation features. Talk about which advertisement does a better job of capturing the intended audience. Be ready to share your ideas.

# AMERICAN CHORE CHAMPION

**S**ure, you can fold laundry… take out the garbage… set the table…but can you do it under pressure, week after week, for cash and prizes, with America watching?

**Finally,** a reality show where incredibly neat kids can really strut their stuff… and you VOTE to decide who survives to clean another week!

**AMERICAN CHORE CHAMPION**
Coming this Fall on the WK Network
Tuesdays and Wednesdays @ 8:00 p.m.
www.wk.com/americanchorechampion

## The Origami Network
*proudly presents:*
*Fold This!!*
**A new show!**

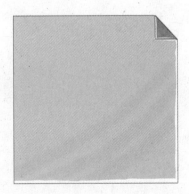

CALL YOUR CABLE PROVIDER AND CHECK OUT OUR WEB SITE.

## Presentation Matters

Imagine that you have been given the job of designing a poster for your school's upcoming winter carnival. It's a big deal. There will be games, live music, food, and fun. The purpose of the carnival is to raise money for a cause your community supports. (You can decide what that is.) Plan to

- create a name for this year's carnival.
- identify important informational points to emphasize.
- create an eye-catching visual for your poster.

**Note:** You do not need to be a great artist or graphic designer. It's fine to import art from the Internet or borrow photos from a publication, as long as you cite your sources.

Your success will be measured by the likelihood that people will attend. Use your own paper or poster board to sketch out a plan. Imagine that you will hand this plan to a designer who will create the final poster. You may also, at your teacher's discretion, create your design on the computer.

## Sample Paper 3

### Score for Ideas _____

# A Little Case of the Hiccups

Hiccups can be very annoying, but most cases last only a few minutes. What if a hiccupping fit lasted longer—say, 68 years? The strange case of Charles Osborne is fascinating because of how long his hiccups lasted. But what exactly is a hiccup? What causes them? How can you make them stop (so you won't have to hiccup for most of your life)?

In 1922, when his hiccups started, Charles Osborne might not have known that a hiccup is a sudden contraction of the diaphragm followed by a quick closing of the throat. The diaphragm is a big sheet of muscle spread across your chest and under your lungs. When it contracts, it tightens and pushes air out of your lungs. When it relaxes, air is pulled in. Once in a while, it contracts and relaxes too fast. Then the brain tells the throat to close and shut off the air flow. It's that sudden stopping of the air that makes the familiar hiccup sound.

Several things can cause hiccups. Think about the last time you had them. Maybe you ate too fast. Maybe you drank too much soda through a straw—and gulped some air with it. You can also get them from jumping into a cold lake or taking a cold shower. Even stretching your neck too much can bring on the hiccups. Charles Osborne's case was unusual. Mr. Osborne, a hog farmer, was dragging around a hog to see how heavy it was. He probably strained his diaphragm, setting off the hiccups. (Remember that next time you are curious about your pig's weight!)

There are also several home remedies for hiccups. They include forcefully holding your breath, plugging your nose while sipping water, eating a spoonful of sugar, breathing into a paper bag—or letting someone scare you enough to make you jump. No doubt Mr. Osborne tried them all over the 68 years he was hiccupping.

What became of Charles Osborne, anyway? Hiccups didn't keep him from having a life. He was married twice, fathered eight kids, and lived to be 97. One day, after 68 years of hiccupping, sometimes up to 40 times a minute, he just stopped—for no apparent reason. He died about a year later. If he were alive today, he might tell us to eat and drink slowly, watch out for quick temperature changes, and avoid lifting hogs—unless we wanted to break his record.

## Sample Paper 4
## Score for Ideas _____

# Is Pluto a Planet?

Nine − one = eight. There used to be nine planets, but now there are eight. That's because Pluto has been downgraded out of the premium package, and been sent to the planet minor leagues. Mercury, Venus, Earth, Mars, Jupiter, Saturn, Uranus, Neptune are now considered the only planets in our solar system.

Pluto was discovered in 1930. This is the same year that Walt Disney introduced Pluto the dog, a now famous character and friend of Mickey Mouse. It is not true that the planet was named after the dog. The cartoon character Pluto was named after the planet instead of the other way around. The name Pluto was given to the planet by an eleven-year-old English girl named Venetia Burney. She was really into Greek and Roman mythology. Pluto is the Roman god of the underworld. In Greek mythology, his name is Hades. Venetia's grandfather knew a college professor in England who passed the name on to a friend at the Lowell Observatory in Arizona. This is where the planet Pluto (or former planet Pluto) was first discovered by looking through a giant telescope.

Astronomers now say that Pluto does not fit the newest rules for what makes a planet a regular planet. Pluto is now called a dwarf planet.

# Revising Checklist for Ideas

☐ I chose a writing topic I like, and I'm excited about it. OR . . .

☐ I want to change my topic to _____.

☐ I have all the information I need to make writing easy. OR . . .

☐ I could get more information from _____.

☐ My main idea is focused and manageable. OR . . .

☐ I'm going to shrink it down to this: _____.

☐ Details expand my discussion or story for readers. OR . . .

☐ I need to include details that answer these readers' questions:

_____?

_____?

_____?

☐ I crossed out any filler (unneeded information that interrupts the main message). OR . . .

☐ I didn't have any!

☐ My title hints at the main idea without telling *too* much.

☐ I shared my writing with _____.

That person's rating of my ideas:

| 1 | 2 | 3 | 4 | 5 | 6 |
|---|---|---|---|---|---|

**Note** Don't use this checklist just to compliment yourself—even if your writing is terrific! Use it to plan revisions or additions. Try to see your writing the way a reader who doesn't know you would see it.

Name _____  Date _____

# Revising Checklist for Conventions and Presentation

☐ After writing my draft, I waited at least three days to edit so I could see it "fresh."

☐ I read my writing twice to check for errors—once silently, once aloud.

☐ I looked carefully at these things: ___ capitalization ___ spelling ___ grammar ___ punctuation ___ paragraphing

☐ There are NO distracting errors (even tiny ones) to slow a reader down or get in the way of the message.

☐ I used punctuation to bring out meaning and voice.

☐ I used *italics* to show readers which words to *emphasize* in reading aloud.

☐ I used **boldface** to make important terms stand out.

☐ IF I used dialogue, I started a new paragraph for each new speaker, and

☐ I used quotation marks to mark each speaker's words.

☐ I designed my presentation to catch a reader's eye.

☐ My presentation makes the "informational trail" easy to follow.

☐ I made important information (facts, names, dates, definitions) easy to find.

☐ My presentation will make the message easy to understand and remember.

☐ I shared my writing with _____.

That person's rating of my conventions and presentation:

| 1 | 2 | 3 | 4 | 5 | 6 |

**Note** Good conventions and presentation are a courtesy. After all, *someone* edits every piece of writing that is read. The question is, will that someone be you, the writer? Or will you leave that task to your reader?

# Organization

Imagine a calendar on which the days and months are out of order. How would you ever use it? Imagine shopping in a store in which items are stacked randomly on shelves, potato chips and shampoo mixed in with clothing and sports equipment. How long might it take to find what you need? Order matters in just about everything—including writing. You may have the most interesting details in the world to share, but unless you order them in a way that is both logical and easy to follow, you limit your reader's ability to understand and appreciate your message. On the other hand, if you carefully plan how to begin, where to go next, and how to wrap things up, your readers will feel as if they're on a guided tour.

**In this unit, you'll learn several strategies for organizing writing effectively. In the lessons that follow, you'll have a chance to**

- explore seven organizational designs.

- choose the right design to match the purpose.

- use transitional words to link ideas.

- write an organized, easy-to-follow paragraph.

## Sample Paper 5
## Score for Organization _____

# A Day to Remember

When we finally got to the barbecue a lot of people were already eating. I played croquet. I had never played croquet before, so someone's dad had to explain it to me. The thing I called a hammer, he called a mallet. The little wire hoops are actually called wickets. We drank lemonade, the homemade kind with a LOT of seeds and pulp in it. The kids I played croquet with weren't very good and I won! That was a surprise. Someone brought their Border Collie, and he kept stealing food from everyone's plates. I forget his name, but he was sneaky and very smart. Then the next day we all went sailing on this humongous boat. You could jump off the boat and swim and then climb back up a ladder on the side. My dad caught a fish. I got an outrageous sunburn. Dad had the fish stuffed and mounted on a plaque. It's on a wall in the basement. Now I'm asking my dad to buy us a croquet set. I love that game! The man who explained croquet to me was really patient. That reminds me—I didn't want that dog to steal my food, but he still really made me laugh. I think maybe we should get a dog.

Name _____ Date _____

## Sample Paper 6
## Score for Organization _____

# Chores? No Problem!

I used to think doing chores was worse than being put on the rack, that medieval torture device on which your arms and legs get stretched with ropes. Now I look at them differently. My mom likes to think that I'm maturing and that I understand more about responsibility. Maybe. But the real reason for my new attitude is that my twin younger brothers just turned eight. Happy birthday, Colin and Ryan!

Why is this particular birthday bash such a cause for celebration? It's simple. In our house, turning eight means you are old enough to have chores. My parents also decided (this was one of their best decisions ever) that, being the oldest, I get to assign certain chores—kind of like a "chore manager." You might say that in a way, my brothers now work for me! My dad says I'm supposed to be a good, fair boss. Of course! Fairness is my middle name. Still, this is an incredible opportunity. So I do plan to keep certain chores just for myself, the ones I really don't mind doing—like organizing the recycling, vacuuming, and feeding the cat. In front of my brothers though, I make these chores seem like the worst. I groan. I make faces. They think I'm doing them a favor taking these things off their hands. Meanwhile, my brothers get to collect and sort the laundry, load and empty the dishwasher, and my least favorite, clean the sink and toilet in the bathroom we share. (I might add that this is only fair since eight-year-olds are not especially neat.)

Thursdays and Sundays are chore days at our house. I used to dread those days because they meant a lot of work for me. Now, I kind of look forward to them. I hand out the work assignments with a smile and hum the birthday song while I work.

# Organization

**The WRITER...**
opens with an inviting lead.

**So the READER...**
_____
_____
_____

**The WRITER...**
organizes information to showcase the message.

**So the READER...**
_____
_____
_____

**The WRITER...**
uses helpful transitions.

**So the READER...**
_____
_____
_____

**The WRITER...**
closes with a satisfying conclusion.

**So the READER...**
_____
_____
_____

# name that Design!

**W**hether you are writing the recipe for your grandma's famous turkey noodle soup, composing a newspaper story about a high school basketball team, or describing the Grand Canyon on video, you need an organizational design to hold your ideas together. Details make a message interesting—but an organizational design makes that message easy to follow. As you might expect, different types of writing call for different organizational designs. In this lesson, we'll explore five, and you'll have a chance to imitate one of them in your own writing.

## Five Organizational Designs

Following are brief descriptions of five different ways to organize ideas and information in a piece of writing. There are many others, of course, but these five offer several useful ways of organizing information.

Put a check mark in the box below each design that you have seen as a reader. Put a check mark in the other box if you have also used the design as a writer.

## Chronological Order (Time)

Details are arranged in the order in which they happened (first, second, next, and so on). Most stories are organized this way (with variations, such as flashbacks). Biographical essays, history books, science reports, and many news stories are organized chronologically.

☐ I have seen this design as a reader.

☐ I have used this design as a writer.

## Visual or Spatial Order

Details are described in a way that creates a scene or image in the reader's mind. Descriptions of all kinds are organized spatially. So are some poems! Certain directions—how to assemble a bicycle, for example—combine chronological and spatial order (directions + a diagram).

☐ I have seen this design as a reader.

☐ I have used this design as a writer.

## Order of Importance

Details are arranged from most to least important—or (less often) from least to most important. Persuasive essays, some news stories, and some expository essays are organized in a way that begins with the most important point and then expands to include related points. Some pieces *lead up* to the most important point. That helps make the main point memorable—like a joke's punch line.

☐ I have seen this design as a reader.

☐ I have used this design as a writer.

**Design D**

## Cause and Effect

This design may begin by describing the cause of a problem or situation, then elaborating on the effects. Or the writer may explore several effects first, then go on to reveal the likely cause. Writing that explores or analyzes problems (anything from weight gain to military conflict) is likely to be organized in this way.

☐ I have seen this design as a reader.

☐ I have used this design as a writer.

**Note:** The cause-and-effect and problem-solution designs are closely related. But in the problem-solution design, the writer has a solution in mind and usually wants to convince people to adopt that solution. Persuasive writing often uses the problem-solution design.

**Design E**

## Comparison-Contrast

The writer explains how two or more subjects are alike and different. Often the writer uses one subject that is familiar to most readers (a house cat) and compares it with something less familiar (the Bengal tiger).

☐ I have seen this design as a reader.

☐ I have used this design as a writer.

# Name that Design!

Following are three short paragraphs, each using one of the organizational designs you just read about. As you read each paragraph, decide which design the writer is using.

**Tip:** Mark any keywords in each paragraph that offer clues about the design. Put the letter of your choice on the line.

Ⓐ Chronological Order          Ⓓ Cause and Effect

Ⓑ Visual or Spatial Order      Ⓔ Comparison-Contrast

Ⓒ Order of Importance

Name _____    Date _____

**Example 1**

Since the attack on the World Trade Center and the Pentagon on September 11, 2001, airport security has been extra tight. Beefed-up security means longer lines at ticket counters and security checkpoints. If a person is not a ticketed passenger, he or she can no longer say goodbye to friends and family at the gate—or greet them as they first get off the plane. Some airport businesses have had to shut down due to slower pedestrian traffic. It's all part of the new security program.

**Organizational Design** _____

**Example 2**

When we reached the top of the mountain, the view took my breath away. Directly in front of us stretched miles of trees, rocks, and hills. Along the horizon, we could see the ocean and miles of blue. Straight down from where we stood was a several-hundred-foot drop-off, and at the bottom of that, a pile of rather jagged-looking rocks. As we turned in any direction, the view would change from one amazing scene to another.

**Organizational Design** _____

**Example 3**

Weekends are supposed to be for rest and play, aren't they? Yet increasing numbers of Americans are reportedly more tired on Monday morning than on Friday night—the traditional end of the workweek. Many people do not sleep regular hours on weekends; they're too busy having fun! Moreover, people tend not to eat regular meals during busy weekends, and what they do eat is often junk food. Between Friday and Sunday evening, people crowd in too many activities: visiting friends and family, running errands, and catching up on chores. But what is most significant is that "no-rest" weekends are cutting into productivity. People simply cannot work as hard or as efficiently when they're exhausted.

**Organizational Design** _____

## Share and Compare

Meet with a partner to compare your choices. Did you see and hear the same design in each example? Look back at the definitions as you discuss any disagreements.

# Two Important Choices

As a writer, you want to be comfortable with many organizational designs. That way you can choose the right design to match your writing purpose.

### Choice 1

Of course, you don't begin with the design. You begin with the message. So let's focus on the message first. Is there a topic on which you could write one or two paragraphs right now? If so, jot your idea down here:

_____

_____

_____

If no idea pops into your head, consider one of ours—or use our list to help you think of an idea of your own:

- Living in your neighborhood versus living somewhere else
- What to do if you become lost in the forest or city
- A view you especially love
- How life at school changes from elementary to middle school

Name _____     Date _____

Choice 2

With a topic in mind, which organizational design do you think you are most likely to use? Why?

_____

_____

_____

Keep in mind that you may change your mind as you write, and you may also use more than one design in a given piece. Writers often do!

## Designing Your Writing

Use your own paper for this. Remember to take time to plan and prewrite. Think about your organizational design and, if it helps, create a list or graphic that helps you picture that design. You might

- draw a sketch.
- make a web.
- make a list.

When you feel ready, write for 10 to 15 minutes. Keep your pencil moving the entire time, if possible. Remember to include a strong lead that gets readers excited and a good ending that wraps things up.

## Share and Compare

Meet with a partner or in a writing circle to share your paragraphs. Listen carefully to each piece of writing. Can you hear the design? How does it help you follow the message? Write the name of the design you hear on a note card, fold it, and pass it to the writer when he or she finishes reading. (Don't peek at these cards until everyone has shared.) Does the design your readers/listeners hear match what you think you used?

Name _____     Date _____

## ? A Writer's Questions

Many writers follow an overall design, such as chronological order, but they wind up weaving many other sorts of organizational designs into parts of their writing as they work. Why would this be? How many designs might you find in, say, a mystery novel? How about a history textbook?

## Putting It to the Test

It's pretty clear that if you are taking a writing test, having a well-organized story or essay will help you. But when time is limited, how will you get started? Is there a quick sketch, graphic, list, or other sort of planning you might do on scratch paper to help you think through each of the five designs discussed in this lesson? Discuss them with the class.

# Writing by Design

**A**musement parks are designed differently from shopping malls or housing developments. Similarly, hotels have one sort of design, airports another, and schools yet another. Good design always reflects function, or purpose. That holds true in writing, too (as you discovered with the short piece you wrote at the end of the last lesson). Good writers narrow their topics, think about which details will amuse or educate readers, and then design the flow of ideas to make the message easy to understand and interesting to read.

## Jogging Your Memory

In the previous lesson, we looked at five common organizational designs. How many of those five can you recall without looking back? List them here. It's fine to talk with a partner as you make your list:

**A.** _____

**B.** _____

**C.** _____

**D.** _____

**E.** _____

Did you recall all five? Good for you, if you did! Now, with your class, see if you can think of two or more kinds of writing that would follow each of those designs.

## Adding Two More

As we noted earlier, there are several ways to organize writing. We have explored five. Now we'll add two more—also chosen because they are common and useful.

### Design F

**Step-by-Step**

The writer explains to the reader, step-by-step, how to do something—or sometimes, how something happens. Such a design could work for directions on making soup or tying a fly (for a fishing rod). It could also be used to explain how metamorphosis occurs or what happens during a heart attack.

☐ I have seen this design as a reader.

☐ I have used this design as a writer.

### Design G

**Main Idea and Support**

The writer has a main point to make and uses examples, facts, or anecdotes (short stories) to support that point. This design works with many types of informational writing, reviews of books or films, and persuasive essays.

☐ I have seen this design as a reader.

☐ I have used this design as a writer.

# Match Them Up!

Following are seven writing tasks you might encounter. Carefully read and consider each one. Choose a design (A through G) you think would work well. Think about the purpose and audience for each task. Work with a partner.

**Task 1:** Description of your favorite painting from the art museum field trip

**Audience:** Your teacher

**My main organizational design:**

_____

**Task 2:** Diary of your week at an outdoor school

**Audience:** Fifth graders who will attend next year

**My main organizational design:**

_____

**Task 3:** An opinion paper about whether the school day should be lengthened

**Audience:** Your local school board

**My main organizational design:**

_____

**Task 4:** A campaign speech supporting a particular candidate

**Audience:** Your classmates

**My main organizational design:**

_____

**Task 5:** A newspaper article about the mysterious vandalizing of playground equipment

**Audience:** Students at your school

**My main organizational design:**

_____

**Task 6:** An essay about which is more challenging—skiing or snowboarding

**Audience:** Your uncle, a devoted skier

**My main organizational design:**

_____

**Task 7:** An explanation of how raising the price of hot lunches will help solve a school's budget problems

**Audience:** Your principal

**My main organizational design:**

_____

## Share and Compare

Meet with another team to compare choices. For each of the seven writing tasks, be prepared to explain why you made the choice you did. Did the intended audience have any effect on your choice? Is it possible to have more than one right answer for a particular writing task?

# The Two-Minute Conference

As you know by now, good organization begins not with design but with the message—something to say. You need to choose a design that fits your purpose, not vice versa. In choosing topics, let's try a form of prewriting that works for many writers: talking. Have a two-minute conference with your partner. Ask questions—and offer suggestions. Use your two minutes to talk about the following.

- What's on your mind right now that you could write about
- Ways you like to spend your free time
- Things you enjoy—and things that annoy you
- What matters to you right now
- Things you like (or do not like) writing about

Then write your topic here: _____

## Writing by Design

Once you have your topic in mind, take another minute or two to plan. You might

- make a list of questions to answer.
- make a web, putting your topic in the center.
- draw a quick sketch.
- just think silently about your topic, eyes closed, mind focused.

Name

Date

Choose an organizational design you think is a good fit for your topic. Write it here:

_____

Using your own paper, write for 10 to 15 minutes on your topic, guiding your reader right through your thinking. Keep the pencil moving!

## A Writer's Questions

Look at any piece of writing from your folder, rough or final draft. What organizational design did you use? It's possible that you used more than one.

_____

_____

Do you feel you chose the best design for your purpose, or would you make a different choice based on what you know now?

## Putting It to the Test

In a testing situation, do you think it would help or hurt your score if your organizational design were obvious to the reader who scores your paper? In other words, should the design be obvious and stand out? Or should the reader's attention be focused more on the writer's ideas?

# Building Bridges

**I**magine each sentence in a paragraph as an island and each paragraph in a longer piece as a group of islands. If the writer doesn't build "bridges" connecting these islands, readers may feel stranded.

Skilled writers use specific words and phrases to build word bridges from one sentence, paragraph, or section of writing to the next. These word bridges, also called **transitions,** make it easier for a reader to follow the writer's thoughts. They include words and expressions such as *for example, the next day, however, on the other hand, to illustrate, later that night,* and so on. Such expressions help the reader make the leap from one idea to the next.

Name

Date

# Sharing an Example: *Voyage of a Summer Sun*

In this example of writing, author Robin Cody has carefully selected transitions to help readers see what he is seeing from his canoe. The transitions in this paragraph help show place, location, or direction. The writer uses them to paint a kind of visual panorama.

Take turns reading this passage aloud with a partner. Do NOT look at the passage while your partner reads. You will hear it with and without transitions:

- The first reader should leave out the highlighted transitions.
- The second reader should include them.

A light breeze came from the south, bending lake reeds in the direction I wanted to go, up the west shore. Across the narrow lake, timber furred the slope. On top, snowcapped pinnacles of Rockies appeared only in the bare-rock gaps between nearer mountains. On my side of the lake, sheer sandstone cliffs leveled off to a high bench of hay fields and horse pasture. The highway rode the bench, out of sight and sound. Columbia Lake was all mine. I saw no other person, no other boat, all morning. From holes in white sandstone, blue-backed swallows dived at the canoe and veered away. Puffed clouds bunched at peaks east and west, but the sky above stayed blue and the lake took on a deep, Scope green close to shore.

*Voyage of a Summer Sun*
by Robin Cody

Name                                 Date

# The Jump-Start Chart

There are many kinds of transitions or connecting words.
Here's a small list to give you an idea. Notice that they are
grouped by purpose. Read through the list with a partner
and fill in the blanks to show the kind of connection each
group of transitions makes. The first one has been done for
you.

**Here are some transitions that**

• **add an idea:**

and, also, what's more, furthermore, in addition, plus, besides

• _____

above, behind, by, near, next to, across, below, down, off to the
right, far in the distance, in the back of, just beyond, nearby,
over the hill

• _____

after a while, during, eventually, meanwhile, at the same time,
first, second, next, after that, soon, then, this afternoon,
yesterday, last year, next month, tomorrow

• _____

likewise, in comparison, similarly, in the same way, just as, also,
equally, correspondingly

• _____

because, as a result, consequently, so, therefore, for that reason

• _____

but, still, on the other hand, however, yet, on the contrary,
to see it another way, nevertheless, in contrast,
from another perspective

• _____

for example, to illustrate, as one example, for instance,
as ____ points out

# Searching for Transitions

Following is a short passage in which the writer makes good use of transitional words and phrases. Work with a partner to see how many you can find. Remember, you are looking for words that connect one idea to another. Feel free to look back at the transitions chart. (Some transitions in this passage may not be on the chart.) Use a highlighter to mark any transitions you find.

**HINT:** Sometimes a transition comes in the middle of a sentence.

### Future Star

From the time he was five, Mario had wanted to play football. At first he was content to play with his two older brothers, Emilio and Jorge. For two years they practiced with him in the backyard. Even when he fell or got hurt, Mario never let out a whimper. As time went on, though, Mario outgrew the backyard. He wanted space. Because he was so tough, they finally relented and took him down to the regular football field to play. They didn't expect too much. After all, Mario was only seven. He surprised them, however, when he made every catch. They thought he would get tired, but he didn't. They also thought he'd get bored with all the running and catching, but he didn't. What's more, he could outrun Emilio, who was ten! After that day, they never teased Mario. They knew that eventually, he'd be a star.

## Share and Compare

Your teacher will now lead you through the passage. Coach him or her as you mark the transitions together. Mark any words or phrases you missed. You may have found some transitional language that no one else did.

How did you and your partner do?

☐ We found many transitions. We totally get this!

☐ We found a few transitions, and now we have a better idea what to look for.

☐ We did not find any transitions. Help!

☐ We thought we found transitions, but the words we marked were not really transitional words or phrases. Help!

# Building Bridges from Scratch

Now it's your turn to build bridges. You'll select transitions—words *or* phrases—to help this piece of writing make sense. Carefully read the passage below with a pencil in hand. If a needed transition is missing, add it. If you find a transition that doesn't make sense, cross it out and replace it with one that makes the connection clear.

**HINT:** Change the wording of any sentences if it helps make your transitions smoother.

The news report said there could be snow in the morning. However, I found my boots, gloves, and hat. Nevertheless, I ran upstairs to tell my sisters the good news. For example, I told my brother the good news also. He was pretty excited, however, about the possibility of having a day off from school. On the other hand, my sisters were pretty happy about having a chance to play in the snow! My mom was the only one who did not think that a snow day would be fun. In conclusion, she would be the only one who wouldn't get a real day off. Therefore, she'd wind up making lunch for three restless kids. We kept our celebration to ourselves.

Name

Date

## A Writer's Questions

Have you taken a close look lately at the kinds of transitions you've been using in your own writing? Choose one piece from your folder, and read it aloud to yourself. Mark any places that seem to be missing transitions, and revise any that are not as strong as they could be. How did you do?

☐ I did not revise anything. My transitions were very strong.

☐ I revised by changing/adding one or two new transitions.

☐ I made a ton of revisions by changing/adding several transitions. The bridges are much stronger now.

## Putting It to the Test

People who score student essays in writing assessments are often known to say, "I don't see how this writer got from Point A to Point B!" What do you suppose they mean by this? How could clear, carefully chosen transitions help?

# Putting It All Together

Several things go into good organization. They include

- a dynamite lead that grabs readers and won't let go.
- a design that fits your purpose.
- transitions that link ideas so readers "get the connections."
- a strong conclusion that wraps everything up.

Think you can put all the pieces together? Here's your big chance! For this lesson, we chose a topic and did a little research to jump-start your writing. As always, you are welcome to choose your own topic—but you will need to do some research if you do. Ready? Let's get organized!

## What's the Big Idea?

Coral snakes. Well, that's the big idea for today, anyhow. It's actually TOO BIG—and you know what that means . . .

On the next page you will find a list of 14 facts about coral snakes. Read through the list carefully, and see if you can narrow down the topic from "coral snakes" to something more manageable. Ask yourself questions like the following.

What's unique about coral snakes?

Where would I find a coral snake?

How do coral snakes defend themselves?

Name _____    Date _____

## Research Facts and Details

_____ **1.** Australia has many poisonous snakes.

_____ **2.** The coral snake is highly venomous, and its bite can be deadly to humans.

_____ **3.** Lizards and other small snakes are the coral snake's main source of food.

_____ **4.** Many people fear snakes.

_____ **5.** Coral snakes are usually rather shy.

_____ **6.** They spend most of their lives buried in the soil or burrowed under rocks.

_____ **7.** Coral snakes are not considered aggressive.

_____ **8.** Coral snakes usually have a black snout and red, yellow, black, and white bands.

_____ **9.** Some snakes are considered mimics of the coral snake.

_____ **10.** If you try to hold or restrain a coral snake, it will try to bite.

_____ **11.** They have small heads, which makes it hard to hold them behind the head.

_____**12.** To tell the real coral snake from a mimic snake, remember this rhyme:

"Red and yellow, kill a fellow; red and black, friend of Jack."

yellow-red-yellow = coral snake
red-black-red = mimic snake

_____**13.** If threatened, the coral snake may flatten its body to look larger.

_____**14.** There are many different kinds of snakes in the world.

**My new whittled down, focused topic:**

_____

## Keep or Toss?

Imagine yourself at an informational store with a cart labeled "My Topic." What do you want to put in your cart, and what do you want to leave on the shelf? Let your focused topic be your guide. If a detail helps you write about your topic, it goes in the cart. If not, it doesn't make the cut.

Read the list of "Research Facts and Details" a second time. This time,

- circle the number beside any detail you want to include in your writing.
- put an X over the number of any detail you want to leave out.

**Hint:** Information that is too general, not interesting enough, or not connected to your topic should be tossed!

## Create Some Order

Notice those little blanks to the left of each detail? Use those to renumber the facts and details you kept. Number them in the order in which you want to write about them.

## Choose a Design

What kind of organizational design would fit your topic?
Remember, it all depends on your message. Here are some
ideas—but you may have a design that fits your message
better. Organizational designs are like shoes—they fit best
when you pick them out yourself.

### 1. Comparison-Contrast

Use this design to compare the coral snake to
another creature.

### 2. Visual or Spatial Order

Use this design for a description.

### 3. Cause and Effect

Use this design to explain what causes a snake to
bite—and the effects of that bite.

### 4. My own design idea: _____

Depending on your message, many other designs
are possible!

## Grab that Reader's Attention!

What if your readers don't know much about coral snakes—
or think this topic isn't very interesting? Imagine that! It's up
to you to write a lead that will change their minds and make
them want to learn even more. Do that now, using your own
paper. When you're happy with your lead, keep writing for
15 minutes or more.

**Hint:** Use one of your best details for your lead. Save
another for the conclusion. Your ending should leave the
reader with something to think about.

Name _____ Date _____

## Share and Compare

Share your paragraph with a partner or in a writing circle. Listen carefully for the following elements, and offer any comments that could help the writer.

- A strong lead
- An organizational design that fits the topic
- Strong transitions (word bridges) to keep ideas connected
- A thoughtful conclusion that wraps up the topic

Jot down the organizational strength of each writer's piece on a note card and fold it in half. Hand it to the writer, but do not open any of them until everyone has shared!

### A Writer's Questions

What do you find most difficult in organizing? Writing a strong lead? Deciding which details to keep or toss? Putting details in order? Using transitions? Writing a conclusion? Find a book by a favorite writer. What does he or she do?

### Putting It to the Test

Suppose you are writing your essay on coral snakes for a writing assessment, and you have 35 minutes to put the piece together. You have to pull facts and details from memory. You also need to decide on a main message, choose a good design, write a strong lead, and so on. Try to visualize yourself in this position. Then make a plan. On scratch paper, make a vertical list with seven 5-minute slots of time. (Just number 1 through 7.) Make notes to show how you would fill each 5-minute slot. Discuss the results with your class. Who came up with the best plan?

## Conventions and Presentation
## Editing Level 1: Conventions

# TOC: A Treasure Map

**W**hat is the best way to find out how a textbook, magazine, or other document is organized? Simple. Open it to the TOC: table of contents. A complete TOC offers a preview of coming attractions. It also helps readers navigate a publication and quickly find the precise chapter or section that will best answer their questions. Without such a guide, searching for information could eat up valuable time and create considerable frustration. An organized TOC is a gift from writers to readers, like a secret map that leads to hidden treasures.

## A Warm-Up

With your teacher's help, take a few minutes to look through the TOCs of various publications. Notice how various TOCs are set up and the kinds of information they contain. Where do you find the following items?

- Preface
- Foreword
- Acknowledgments
- Introduction

- Index
- List of sources
- Glossary

Use the chart below to make a list of some of the elements you find in more than one TOC, and jot down where you find each one (beginning, middle, end of the TOC).

### Table of Contents

| Elements | Location Notes |
|---|---|
| 1. | |
| 2. | |
| 3. | |
| 4. | |
| 5. | |

## Share and Compare

Compare your chart with a partner's. Did you list similar elements? Were your location notes consistent with your partner's? Add anything to your chart that your partner noticed but you did not.

# Random Order = A Problem for Readers

Following is an example TOC from a fictitious piece of writing. As you'll see, it has a little problem. The elements are out of order and, for readers, that means trouble. Imagine that this writer has asked you for help in making this TOC useful for readers. Can you put things in order? You can number the elements in the blanks provided or rewrite them on scratch paper.

**Note:** Chapter and page numbers are not provided since they would have made this task much too easy.

### Hug a Slug

### by S. Limy

____ Index

____ How to befriend slugs

____ Introduction by
Dr. Gastro Podd

____ **Part II—Pests or Pals?**

____ Resources

____ Slug habitat, range,
and diet

____ Slugs in my
garden—help!

____ **Part I—Slugs
From A-Z**

____ Author's Note

____ Acknowledgments

____ What is a slug?

____ Appendix

____ How to control
slugs

____ How slugs move

## Share and Compare

Compare your TOC with your partner's. Are they an exact match? If there are differences, ask yourself if each TOC's organization makes sense and seems a logical match for the topic.

### A Writer's Questions

Writers need to know just what to include in a TOC. Would it be possible, for example, to make a TOC too skimpy, leaving out important things? Would it be possible to overdo and include too much information, having an entry for every paragraph? How does a writer know when he or she has hit the right balance?

# Preparing to Publish

**n**ot *everything* you write will require a TOC. But if your writing is long and complex, or if it is separated into sections, a TOC will be enormously helpful to readers—provided it's set up well. Strong presentation is essential for readers to find information quickly and easily.

## A Warm-Up

With the help of your teacher or librarian, revisit some of the publications you explored earlier. This time, look for a TOC that has appealing layout or presentation. Consider font choice and size, alignment, spacing, art visuals, use of color, or any other presentation elements used to attract and direct the reader's eye. Is there a visual theme that connects the TOC to the book's topic? Can you also find a TOC that does not work well visually? Can you say why? Imagine you are going to teach a lesson on how to set up a TOC. With your partner, find one strong and one weak example to use in your lesson.

## Presentation Practice

### To Publish or Not to Publish

A publisher is deciding whether to publish a book for young adults on keeping their rooms clean and orderly. (Sounds like a best seller.) So far, the writer has only turned in the following TOC. Based on this information, what can you tell about this book? What suggestions would you make to the author about the TOC specifically? What about the content of the book?

# Let's Clean Up!
# Table of Contents

On a scale of 1 to 10, with 10 being "a sure thing" and 1 representing "not a chance," what are the odds this book will get published? Circle your answer.

| 1 | 2 | 3 | 4 | 5 | 6 | 7 | 8 | 9 | 10 |

## A Writer's Question

What hints about content or style does a TOC offer to readers?

# Presentation Matters

Look again at the rough TOC you created for the hypothetical book *Hug a Slug*. Take your editing to the next level—presentation—by entering that TOC on the computer and designing the layout to make it attractive. You may do anything you like, but be sure that at a minimum you attend to the following features.

- Choose a font style and size

- Decide whether to use more than one font

- Decide whether to put any elements in ALL CAPS

- Decide whether some elements will be in **bold** print or *italic* print

- Include page numbers (make these up), presented properly

- Decide whether to use illustrations of any kind

- Choose colors for fonts and background

- Place the entire TOC on the page to create a balanced look

**Sample Paper 7**

**Score for Organization** _____

# The Bouncing Czech

*"Why should I practice running slow? I already know how to run slow. I want to learn to run fast."*

*"If you want to win something, run 100 meters. If you want to experience something, run a marathon."*

These are the words of Emile Zátopek, the "Bouncing Czech," one of the greatest distance runners of all time. He was also known as "The Locomotive" because he ran by his opponents like a train during his career from 1948 to 1955. In his lifetime he won four Olympic gold medals and one silver medal. This Czechoslovakian-born runner will probably be best remembered for how he changed the way distance runners train—and for his amazing accomplishments at the 1952 Olympics in Helsinki, Finland.

Emile Zátopek was born in Czechoslovakia in 1922. He wasn't one of those kids who dreamed of becoming an Olympic runner from the time he could first walk. His first race didn't happen until he was sixteen years old and the shoe company where he worked was sponsoring a 1500-meter race (1500 meters is just a little short of one mile). Emile wasn't a trained runner, and he had to be talked into taking part. Remarkably, this person who had to be coaxed into competing came in second out of 100 runners. At that point, he began to think seriously about running.

Only four years later, in 1944, Emile broke the Czech records for the 2000, 3000, and 5000 meters. In 1948, he ran in his first Olympics, where he won the 10,000 meters (6.2 miles) and placed second in the 5000 meters. During a stretch following the 1948 Olympics, Emile won 38 straight 10,000m races. "The Locomotive" was rolling, full steam ahead.

Emile's training methods seemed strange to other runners at the time. Even though he was a distance runner, his training involved practices that sprinters used. He would run full speed for certain distances. But he combined this with running at slower speeds, jogging, and even walking. This kind of interval training is used in some form by almost all high-level runners today. What's more, it may well have been this kind of training that eventually led Emile to his greatest achievement.

In the 1952 Olympics in Helsinki, Finland, Emile Zátopek went against his doctor's orders and competed in three difficult events. In spite of a gland infection that lasted more than eight days, Emile competed in the 5,000m, 10,000m, and the marathon, and amazingly won each event. He had never even run a marathon before, yet he won the 26-plus-mile event. Even more amazing, Emile set world records in each of these events. The inspiring finish to his 5,000m race can be seen in an online video. At one point during the last lap of the race, Emile is running in fourth place. His face grimacing with pain, he pushes by all the runners to win the gold medal.

Emile Zátopek will always be honored for his Olympic achievements and for the way he changed how runners train. After winning his first marathon in Helsinki, Emile said, "I was unable to walk after that, so much did the race take out of me. But it was the most pleasant exhaustion I have ever known." How fortunate that someone encouraged Emile to run in his first race all those years ago.

## Sources

"Profiles: Emile Zátopek." Running Past. Running Past LLC. 14 October 2009   <http://www.runningpastcom/emil_zatopek.htm>.

"Zátopek Wins 5,000 meter in the 1952 Olympics." 14 October 2009 <http://www.youtube.com/watch?v=3Irnx6Upmkg>.

Name _____    Date _____

## Sample Paper 8
## Score for Organization _____

# Basketball: A Dangerous Sport

There are a lot of dangerous sports in the world. Here are five that are pretty dangerous. In fact you could die doing any of the following sports even if you do things right.

- BASE jumping
- Cave diving
- Bull riding
- Street luging

Some of these dangerous sports are not that well known or common. BASE jumping is when people wearing a parachute jump from buildings, antennae, spans (bridges), and earth (cliffs). What some people don't know is that bicycling is a pretty dangerous sport, and it's done by a lot of people. It's really dangerous when people don't wear helmets.

Basketball is a dangerous sport played by millions of people of all ages. Even little kids play basketball. The ball is not what makes it dangerous. It's not the speed that makes it dangerous. It's the jumping, stopping, turning, pivoting, and changing speed and direction that make it dangerous.

Last year, more people went to hospital emergency rooms for basketball injuries than for football, soccer, skateboarding, volleyball, golf, or wrestling.

### Sources

Carey, Bjorn. "The Most Dangerous Sports in America." *Live Science.* 14 June 2006 <http://www.livescience.com/health/060614_sport_injuries.htm.>.

Name _____    Date _____

# Revising Checklist for Organization

☐ My lead sets the stage and gets your attention! OR

☐ I should begin with: _____ .

☐ My ending wraps things up and leaves you thinking. OR

☐ I should end with: _____ .

☐ This writing is easy for readers to follow. They will NEVER feel lost.

☐ I stayed with ONE main message or story, beginning to end.

☐ I have a surprise or two—not everything is completely predictable.

☐ Details and events seem to come at just the right moment.

☐ I would describe my overall design this way:

_____

_____

☐ I used paragraphs to show small shifts in the story or discussion.

☐ I shared my writing with _____

That person's rating of my organization:

| 1 | 2 | 3 | 4 | 5 | 6 |

**Note** Good organization guides your reader through your writing as if you were shining a light on a dark path in the forest. Did you shine a light on the trail of your thinking—or leave readers in the dark?

# Voice

Writer and teacher Donald Murray once said that voice separates writing that is read from writing that is *not* read. He meant that if you want anyone to read what you have written, you had better make sure it has **Voice.**

So . . . what exactly is Voice? You know where to find the lead in a piece of writing. You could highlight a strong verb or a specific detail if you were asked. But if you were asked to point out the voice in a piece of writing, what would you point to?

That's just it. Voice isn't any one thing. It's many things—and like light in a room, it touches every part of your writing. Think of ideas as what you have to say, organization as the arrangement of those ideas on paper, and voice as *how you express yourself.* Maybe you're thinking, "Wait a minute! It sounds like voice is mostly personality. How do I learn to have more personality?" Don't worry. That part of voice is already inside you. You just need to let it out. As you'll discover, writers use many strategies to enhance the trait of Voice, such as writing for a particular audience, researching a topic to gain an insider's perspective, choosing intriguing details, and projecting enthusiasm. Choose a topic you care about, research it well, and *your* voice will find its way onto the paper—guaranteed.

**In this unit you'll discover your own voice as you learn to**

- listen or read for voice.
- identify voice in expository writing.
- match voice with purpose and audience.
- revise to strengthen voice.

Name _____  Date _____

## Sample Paper 9

## Score for Voice _____

# Climbing Rocket Butte

I think climbing Rocket Butte was maybe the hardest thing I have ever done. Or one of the hardest. At least it's the hardest thing I can remember doing. It was a Saturday I'm pretty sure because we didn't have school. My dad, my brother Ben, and I were all going to do the climb. We got up pretty early and stuff because we had to get like this special pass or something for climbing the butte. I think it's about two miles to the top, but you park down below. Then you hike. First, we drove to the trailhead, and we had to show our pass. We parked the car somewhere it looked like there might be shade later. We started to climb. We all brought water bottles, and I wore my hiking shoes. Ben is a pretty good climber. He pretty much ran up the first hill. He's kind of a show off and stuff, being 15. He plays football. After that, I didn't see too much of him because he was always pretty far ahead of me on the trail. Dad stayed near me, but I could tell he wanted to go ahead, too. It was kind of nice to have company at first, but then I kind of ran out of things to say. Plus it is pretty hard to talk when you are out of breath. I mainly wanted to get it over with. Also I had to keep stopping and take a drink or catch my breath. It must have taken me about a couple hours to get to the top, or maybe it wasn't quite that long. I forget. I remember Ben already waving or jumping around or something when I got to the top. I don't know how long it took him. It probably wasn't that long. He's a pretty good climber. We might go again sometime. You can see a lot from up there.

Name _____     Date _____

## Sample Paper 10
## Score for Voice _____

# Parking with Dad

People have their own way of doing things. My dad is no exception. He has his own way of parking, and it's pretty different from Mom's. This would upset Dad if he knew it, so I don't tell him, and I'm sure he assumes Mom drives just the way he does. Ha!

When Mom drives into a parking lot, she takes the first space she finds that is close to the door. This is, I think, the way most people park. Well, not my dad. First, he sizes up the lot—which spots will be hard to back out of, where might he get blocked by a delivery truck, that sort of thing. He avoids those spots, naturally. Then, he looks for shade. Shade is a big plus. However, he won't go for shade if it means giving up safety.

See, my dad has a thing about getting the paint job dinged. He does not like to park close to other drivers or near posts or anything he might hit his door on when getting in and out. Dad also avoids curbs, because they might damage the tires. Parking near the door is the least of my dad's concerns. "You don't mind a little walk, do you?" is his motto. And I don't. Only we park so far away just to avoid other cars, I sometimes wonder why we didn't just walk from home in the first place.

Some days, Dad has trouble find the right spot. Then we have to move several times. When we finally get home, Mom says, "What *took* you guys so long?" Parking, Mom. It's a tough job.

# Voice

**The WRITER...**
gets deeply involved with the topic.

**So the READER...**
_____
_____
_____

**The WRITER...**
speaks in a natural, individual voice.

**So the READER...**
_____
_____
_____

**The WRITER...**
speaks with confidence.

**So the READER...**
_____
_____
_____

**The WRITER...**
thinks about the reader while writing.

**So the READER...**
_____
_____
_____

# Defining Voice

**A** hundred people might tell you their definitions of Voice, but in the end, you need to define this quality for yourself, in your own heart and mind. That definition will guide the voice you put into your own writing. And where does this definition come from? It comes from many places—conversation, hearing gifted speakers, listening to your own thoughts, and above all, from reading. When you can't put a book down, when it seems to echo your innermost feelings, when it makes you tear up or laugh out loud and you can't wait to share it, that's the power of Voice. In this lesson, you'll be part of a writing circle. You'll take turns reading and listening to various voices, and based on what you hear, you'll write a personal definition of Voice.

## First Thoughts

How would you define the trait of Voice right now? **Hint:** Do NOT look at a rubric or checklist for someone else's words. Trust your own heart and mind and write what *you* think.

_____

_____

_____

_____

_____

_____

# Voice

## Voices on Parade

The more you read—published writing, student writing, your own writing—the clearer the concept of Voice will become in your mind. In your writing circle, read each of the following three passages aloud, listening for the writer's voice. Then fill in your response to each voice.

As you read and listen, ask yourself:

1. How does this writing make me feel?

2. Would I like to keep reading—or read this again?

3. Would I share this aloud with a friend, just for fun?

Voice A

I know it's not considered cool to announce to the world that you like bugs, but I don't care. I LOVE INSECTS! There, I said it, using ALL CAPS! That's like shouting. My friends may not be as fond of bugs as I am, but they deal with it. They understand my passion. They have learned not to disrespect insects in front of me—and especially not to squash them. One friend even predicted that I would become a famous entomologist (that's an insect scientist, for those who don't know) and maybe even discover an insect I could name. I even had a special shirt made that says, "BUG me—I don't mind!"

# Voice

On a scale of 1 to 6, Voice A is definitely a . . .

| 1 | 2 | 3 | 4 | 5 | 6 |

Faint whisper . . .
and fading fast

Strong voice that
keeps me reading

I would keep reading if this piece were longer.

☐ Yes, definitely!

☐ Maybe—at least for a page or two.

☐ Are you kidding me? That's enough!

I would read this aloud to a friend.

☐ Yes—this would be fun to read aloud.

☐ No! This is NOT a piece I would share
with anyone.

**Voice B**

It's my job to put out the recycling box and garbage can every Wednesday morning. It's also my job to put them back along the side of the house when I get home from school Wednesday afternoon. I get mad sometimes because the garbage people don't put the lid back on the can carefully. Sometimes it has rolled or been blown almost two houses down. If it has been raining, the can will get water in it. If I don't pour it out, my dad will get mad. This makes me mad. All they have to do is put the lid back on and everything will be OK.

Name _____  Date _____

On a scale of 1 to 6, Voice B is definitely a . . .

| 1 | 2 | 3 | 4 | 5 | 6 |

Faint whisper . . .
and fading fast

Strong voice that
keeps me reading

I would keep reading if this piece were longer.

☐ Yes, definitely!

☐ Maybe—at least for a page or two.

☐ Are you kidding me? That's enough!

I would read this aloud to a friend.

☐ Yes—this would be fun to read aloud.

☐ No! This is NOT a piece I would share with anyone.

### Voice C

There was simply no possible, feasible, rational, or justified way around it. Lisbet Liesel Littleton would have to start delivering newspapers to the McGerren place. Hers was the only route that even came close to the gross old house!

For months she'd been zooming past it at full-bike-velocity, just to get down the block and on with her route. The gloom and doom house was straight out of a monster movie! A rusty wrought iron fence circled the yard, keeping trespassers out . . . or perhaps keeping something *in*. The gates spiked jaggedly at the top and creaked on their hinges in the wind. Wicked, jungle-like grass consumed the yard so that it was impossible to make out much of the house's façade. One particular second-story window was boarded up, a sinister eyepatch. To go barefoot on the rickety wood of the porch would have resulted in splinters, tetanus, the black plague, or worse. And now, out of the wild blue yonder, Mr. McGerren had subscribed?

Name _____ Date _____

Needless to say, it was quite the unpleasant experience having to deliver newspapers there.

Lisbet, ever the professional, had a strict "doormat or free" policy. She vowed to land a doormat shot every time, or she'd knock that issue off the next month's bill.

This meant that for the McGerren house she'd be forced to get off her bike and walk the newspaper up to the splinter-tetanus-plague-inducing porch. Not even the captain of her school's basketball team could have sunk that shot through the wildlife-infested jungle yard.

And so it was that poor little Lisbet Liesel Littleton parked in front of the cringe-worthy old McGerren place and secretly wished, even if it did cost her newspaper sales, that Mr. McGerren would get his news off the Internet like most normal people nowadays.

On a scale of 1 to 6, Voice C is definitely a . . .

| 1 | 2 | 3 | 4 | 5 | 6 |
|---|---|---|---|---|---|

Faint whisper . . .
and fading fast

Strong voice that
keeps me reading

I would keep reading if this piece were longer.

☐ Yes, definitely!

☐ Maybe—at least for a page or two.

☐ Are you kidding me? That's enough!

I would read this aloud to a friend.

☐ Yes—this would be fun to read aloud.

☐ No! This is NOT a piece I would share with anyone.

Name _____ Date _____

## Sharing Personal Choices

Continue your writing circle discussions. Only this time,
share a voice you chose yourself. Read it aloud to the
group with LOTS of expression. Then answer the following
question—with the help of your group:

On a scale of 1 to 6, the voice I chose is about a . . .

| 1 | 2 | 3 | 4 | 5 | 6 |

Faint whisper . . .
and fading fast

Strong voice that
keeps me reading

Here are three words that describe this voice:

1. _____

2. _____

3. _____

## Final Reflection

If you could sound like any writer you heard today, which
one would it be? Why?

_____

_____

_____

_____

_____

_____

## My Personal Definition: Second Thoughts

Look back over the passages, your first thoughts, and your final reflection. Write your own current definition for the trait of Voice on a separate piece of paper.

### Share and Compare

When you have finished, meet in your writing circle with three or four other writers. Take turns reading your definitions. Did anyone think of an aspect of voice you did not think of? Add it if you like!

### A Writer's Questions

Sometimes when a listener hears a lot of voice—or no voice—that person will say, "Well, it's because of the way you are reading." Do you think that's true? Does voice come from the way we read—or does it come from the writing itself?

### Putting It to the Test

Voice often comes from humor. But let's say you are taking a writing test and you are writing about a very serious subject—such as how plastic waste is polluting the oceans of the world. Humor probably feels inappropriate. How then would you manage to write with voice? Should you write with voice about such a topic?

# The Voice of Authority

**A**s a writer, you may feel it's fairly easy to put your voice into a personal narrative. After all, you were *there*. It's *your* story, so you're an authority, right? But let's say you're writing a report on the eastern coral snake. Should you still write knowledgeably? Absolutely. Except, unless you keep coral snakes as pets, you may need to substitute research for first-hand experience. Voice in expository or informational writing comes from the confidence you feel when you know a subject well enough to speak with authority and to choose details your readers will find fascinating. Details are like snacks. Some are great, and some are ho-hum. Readers love to have you serve up some informational tidbits you researched just for their enjoyment. Know your topic inside and out, and you'll be able to do exactly that.

## Reflect and Rate

In your writing circles, share each of the following three samples by reading them aloud and rating them, 1 through 6, together. Talk about which one you like best (or least) and which writers do (or do not) know their topics well enough to write with the "voice of authority."

Example A

### Coral Snakes

"Red and yellow, kill a fellow; red and black, friend of Jack." This little rhyme is a helpful way to tell the difference between a poisonous coral snake and a harmless "mimic" like the scarlet king snake. Even if your name is Matthew or Sarah, knowing the difference could save your life. Coral snakes usually have a black snout followed by a series of red, yellow, white, and black bands. The red bands are always surrounded by yellow bands, which, of course, is your signal to watch out. Not that you're likely to have an encounter with a coral snake. Coral snakes are usually pretty shy, spending most of their time burrowed under a rock or down in the soil. You'd have to try to grab or hold one down before it would try to bite. Coral snakes even have several tricks that make grabbing them as difficult as possible.

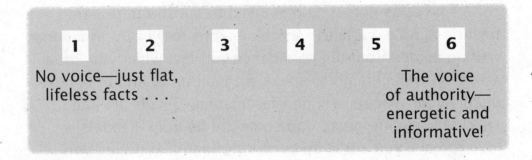

| 1 | 2 | 3 | 4 | 5 | 6 |

No voice—just flat, lifeless facts . . .

The voice of authority— energetic and informative!

## Example B

### Australia

Australia is an island country and the only island continent. Some well-known cities are Sydney, Brisbane, Perth, and Canberra. There are many poisonous and deadly animals in Australia. The world's ten most deadly snakes are native to Australia. There are also sharks, spiders, jellyfish, crocodiles, ticks, and fish that can hurt you. The Great Barrier Reef is located off the coast of Australia. It is considered the world's largest living thing. Ayer's Rock is located in Australia. Its official name is Uluru. It was named by Aborigines, the native people of Australia.

# Voice

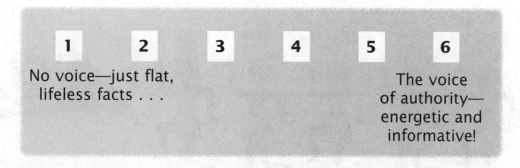

| 1 | 2 | 3 | 4 | 5 | 6 |

No voice—just flat,
lifeless facts . . .

The voice
of authority—
energetic and
informative!

**Example C**

## Khufu: Builder of the Great Pyramid

While the Great Pyramid of Giza, which stood 481 feet tall, is considered one of the Seven Wonders of the World, not much is known about the king who is responsible for it. Even though he ruled for nearly 24 years, the only thing found depicting him is a nine-inch statue. That's pretty ironic for a man who built something so tall. The statue wasn't even found at Giza; it was found in a temple to the south of the Great Pyramid. Khufu's father, Senefru, also a great pyramid builder, was known as a kinder, more benevolent leader than his son. Though he may have been ruthless, Khufu did possess a great ability to organize and lead. Under Khufu's leadership, the pyramid was built without slave labor. Those who worked on the project did so instead of paying taxes.

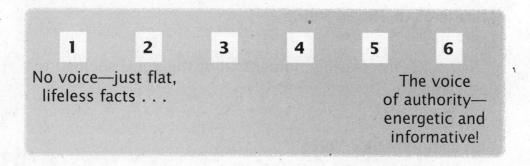

| 1 | 2 | 3 | 4 | 5 | 6 |

No voice—just flat,
lifeless facts . . .

The voice
of authority—
energetic and
informative!

Name _____    Date _____

## Ranking by Voice

Within your writing circles, review your voice ratings for each passage. Then decide which example (A, B, or C) best fits each of the following descriptions. **Hint:** You're ranking the voice behind the information, *not* choosing your favorite topic.

**Strong, Confident Voice**

Example _____

This was the voice of authority—consistent and interesting. I felt I was learning things and could have gone right on reading.

**Middle-of-the-Road Voice**

Example _____

It had some interesting moments, but the voice seemed to come and go.

**Flat-as-a-Pancake Voice**

Example _____

Facts, facts, and *more* facts. Thankfully, it wasn't long.

Name ........................................ Date ........................................

# Revising for Voice: Building Reader Confidence

Which passage did your group rank lowest in voice? Read it again, thinking as a reader. What do you want from this writer? How could he or she reach you? As a group, list three things this writer could do to boost the voice of the passage:

1. _____

2. _____

3. _____

Working together, begin revising the passage by inserting new words or phrases—or rewriting sentences. You can take any information out. You can put any information in. Don't forget the title! Do as much as you can in 15 minutes.

## Share and Compare

When you have finished, be prepared to read your revision aloud to the class. Let them hear your confidence. Pop that voice up to Level 6!

### A Writer's Questions

Many writers are able to put powerful voice into informational writing. Could this have anything to do with the topics they choose to write about? What is the connection? Why would a topic make such a difference?

### Putting It to the Test

In a testing situation, you cannot usually choose your own topic. Someone chooses it for you—or perhaps gives you a choice of two or three topics. How then will you manage to achieve the same voice in your writing as if you'd been able to choose your own topic?

# "Hello" Versus "Wassup"

Imagine telling a friend in another town about New Year's Eve in your neighborhood. You dance and inject a few sound effects as you describe a parade with kids and pets, cars with stereos blaring, or the loud, colorful fireworks that end the celebration. The next day, you find yourself sharing the same story with one of your family's adult friends, who is a stranger to you. Would you use the same words, expressions, and *voice* that you used with your friend? Not likely. Your audience—the person receiving your message— has changed. In writing, audience matters even more than in person because on paper, you don't get to rephrase things. You have to use the right voice for the audience—the very first time.

## Sharing an Example: *Saving Sweetness*

Here is a short example from the humorous book, *Saving Sweetness* by Diane Stanley. In this passage, Mrs. Sump is trying to get the sheriff to do what she wants. Notice the little adjustments she makes as she struggles to find just the right voice for her one-person audience, the sheriff:

Out in the hottest, dustiest part of town is an orphanage run by a female person nasty enough to scare night into day. She goes by the name of Mrs. Sump, though I doubt there ever was a Mr. Sump on accounta she looks like somethin' the cat drug in and the dog wouldn't eat. I heard that Mrs. Sump doesn't much like seein' the orphans restin' or havin' any fun, so she puts 'em to scrubbin' the floor with toothbrushes. Even the ittiest, bittiest orphan, little Sweetness. So one day, Sweetness hit the road.

Name _____ Date _____

I found out right away because Mrs. Sump came bustin' into Loopy Lil's Saloon, hollerin' like a banshee.

"Sheriff!" she yelled (that's me). "That provokin' little twerp—I mean that dear child, Sweetness, done escaped—I mean disappeared! And I'm fit to be tied, worryin' about that pore thang all pink and helpless, wanderin' lost on the plains and steppin' on scorpions and fallin' in holes and such. You gotta bring her back alive—er, I mean safe—before she runs into Coyote Pete!"

*Saving Sweetness*
by Diane Stanley

## Reflecting

Did Mrs. Sump find the right voice to get her way? Look carefully again at the third paragraph. Read it aloud softly to yourself. Then answer these questions:

1. What does Mrs. Sump's natural voice (before she changes it) reveal about her?

   _____

   _____

2. What specific things does Mrs. Sump do to change her voice?

   _____

   _____

3. What sort of new voice does Mrs. Sump hope the sheriff will hear after she adjusts it a bit?

   _____

   _____

Name _____     Date _____

## Different Audience, Different Voice

Imagine that Mrs. Sump is home later that night writing in her diary. (OK, that's a stretch, but let's just pretend she DOES keep one.) Her audience is . . . well, herself! (Unless someone snoops, and who would dare?) That means she can let it all out, saying exactly what she thinks and feels about Sweetness, the sheriff, and the whole situation. Pretend you're Mrs. Sump. Write in her voice for about 3 minutes:

*Dear Diary,*

_____

_____

_____

_____

_____

_____

_____

_____

_____

_____

_____

_____

_____

_____

_____

_____

Name _____  Date _____

## Share and Compare

In your writing circles, share your "Mrs. Sump" voices.
Are they all alike—or slightly different? Is one voice more
wicked than the others? Check any words that apply to
one or more voices in your circle—and add words we didn't
think of. Prepare to share your favorite Mrs. Sump voice
with the class.

- ☐ wicked
- ☐ evil
- ☐ nasty
- ☐ sarcastic
- ☐ unhappy
- ☐ cruel
- ☐ just plain mean
- ☐ misunderstood
- ☐ regretful
- ☐ humorous

Other words we thought of _____

# Writing for Two Audiences

In this part of the lesson, you'll have the chance to adjust
your writer's voice for two different audiences. You are
going to write two notes, one to a friend and the other to
an adult—a teacher or your school principal.

In these letters, give your heartfelt impressions of Voice—
what you have learned, what you enjoy (or dislike) about
studying the trait of Voice, why it's important to writing,
and things your readers should remember to do in their
own writing.

These are not just-for-fun or practice letters. You will really
deliver them to the readers you select. So make sure your
voice is a good match with each reader! Ready? Then, do
the following:

**1.** Meet in your writing circle for 3–5 minutes to make a plan.

**2.** Write your own two letters, using your own paper.

Name _____ Date _____

## Share and Compare

Meet with a partner to take turns sharing your letters. As a test of how well you matched your voice to each reader, don't share the greetings ("Dear Sanjay" or "Dear Principal Casteel") when you read your letters aloud. See whether your partner can tell which letter is for a friend and which is intended for an adult audience.

### A Writer's Questions

Even though you adjust your voice for the intended audience, it's still always you. Are there certain things about your voice that never change, no matter who your reader is? If so, what would those elements be?

### Putting It to the Test

In a testing situation, you only know your audience in the most general way. You have no way to know if the person who reads your writing will be male or female, how old he or she will be, or many other details about them. Professional writers don't know these things, either. So some—like writer/teacher Mem Fox—write for a watcher, a hypothetical person whom the writer pictures in his or her mind. Could this work in a testing situation? Who would your watcher be?

# From Flat to Fantastic

**W**hen you experience strong, voice-filled writing, the words flood your mind with mental pictures and your heart with emotions. You may feel so connected to writing that you cannot stop reading. You may even feel compelled to share it with a friend. Writing that is weak in Voice, on the other hand, leaves you feeling disconnected and uninvolved. So—what does one piece of writing have that the other does not? In this lesson, you'll have a chance to think about that and to turn a piece of flat, voiceless writing into something readers can't put down.

## Starting Strong: *Bull Run*

Writing that is strong in Voice gives off its own energy—in the form of humor, sadness, outrage, confidence, joy, enthusiasm, or plain old curiosity. When writing lacks this energy, readers have to do all the work. Have you ever pretended you were having a good time when you really weren't? Putting your own energy into someone else's writing is a lot like that. It's exhausting.

Look carefully at this passage from *Bull Run* by Paul Fleischman. *Bull Run* tells the story of the Civil War through the voices of 16 different people: male, female, old, young, black, white, northern, southern. This passage is narrated by Fleischman's character Toby Boyce. As you read, ask yourself whether you feel

- energized by the writer's words, OR . . .
- worn out from the writer's lack of energy.

I was eleven years old and desperate to kill a Yankee before the supply ran out. It seemed that all Georgia had joined except me. I knew I'd never pass for eighteen. You can't very well lie about your height. Then I heard that musicians were needed to play for the soldiers, any age at all. I hotfooted it fifteen miles to the courthouse and took my place in line. The recruiter scowled when I reached the front. "You're a knee baby yet," he said. "Go on home." I told him I meant to join the band. "And what would your instrument be?" he asked. My thinking hadn't traveled that far. "The fife," I spoke out. Which was a monstrous lie. He smiled at me and I felt limp with relief. Then he stood up and ambled out the door. Across from the courthouse a band had begun playing. We all heard the music stop of a sudden. A few minutes later the recruiter returned. He held out a fife. "Give us 'Dixie,'" he said. I felt hot all over. Everyone waited. The fife seemed to burn and writhe in my hand like the Devil's own tail.

*Bull Run*
by Paul Fleischman

## Quick Reflection

How much energy did you feel in this passage?

| 1 | 2 | 3 | 4 | 5 | 6 |
|---|---|---|---|---|---|
| None! I had to do ALL the work! | | | | | A lot! It's alive with energy! |

Name                                                    Date

## Get the Voice Out!

What if we rewrote this passage (apologies to Mr. Fleischman), draining out most of Toby Boyce's voice? What would we need to do, exactly? We'll rewrite the first few lines to get you started. Then, meet with your writing circle to see how much more you can do. Remember—this time, NO VOICE ALLOWED! Here we go . . . into the world of the flat and dull . . .

I was eleven years old and wanted to join the army. Lots of other people had joined. I knew I didn't look eighteen. I was too short. Then I heard that musicians could get in. They were needed to play for the soldiers. I went to the courthouse and got in line. The person frowned and told me to go home because I was too young. I told him I wanted to join the band. _____

_____

_____

_____

_____

_____

_____

## Quick Reflection

What did you actually DO to cut out the voice? See if you and your writing circle can think of at least three things you changed.

1. _____

2. _____

3. _____

## Highlighting the Top 5 Moments

Go back now to Fleischman's original passage. With your writing circle members, highlight or underline the Top 5—that is, the five moments in the passage that you think have the MOST voice. Take time to discuss them—you may not all agree at first!

Now, as a group, see if you can identify from one to five things that Fleischman did to create Toby's voice in the passages you highlighted. Be as specific as you can.

**Author Paul Fleischman . . .**

1. _____

2. _____

3. _____

4. _____

5. _____

**Do two more things!**

• Put a star by the strategy you think is MOST important.

• Circle the number of any strategy you'd like to try in your own writing.

## Reversing Gears: *"Greenway Forest"*

You just finished taking the voice *out* of a piece—sort of like letting the air out of a tire . . . SSSsssssssst. Flat.

Now we're going to switch gears. You get to put the voice *in*. Remember all those little tricks that Paul Fleischman used to give his writing energy? Use those—or any others you can think of—to put some life into the passage "Greenway Forest." Edit this piece any way you want, then use the space below for your revision.

It was a pretty day for walking in Greenway Forest. It was a good name for the forest because everything in it was green. I sat down, and leaned against a tree. I almost fell asleep because it was quiet.

I'm so bored with these stories...

Then I heard something. It was coming from behind a bush. At first I thought it was one thing, then I thought it was something else.

Then something came out of the bush. It was a porcupine. He looked at me. He rose up on his hind legs. Then he moved away. I decided to see where he would go.

_____

_____

_____

_____

_____

_____

_____

_____

_____

_____

_____

# Voice

## Share and Compare

Meet with a partner or in writing circles to share your
revised pieces. Have one person read the original aloud first.
Then listen carefully to each revision. Make notes on the
kinds of things other writers did to add voice. Be prepared
to share those observations as a class.

### A Writer's Questions

Is there one big secret to writing with voice? Or are
there many different things a writer can do? Do you
think your way of defining this trait will change
over time?

### Putting It to the Test

Paul Fleischman probably chose to write about the
Civil War because he finds it fascinating. He also
likes creating the voices of multiple characters.
In a testing situation, you do not always have
the freedom to make these kinds of choices. The
topic is chosen for you. Author and teacher Barry
Lane suggests pretending that the topic IS your
favorite—and that you are the world's leading
authority on that topic. How might that strategy
help you put voice into your writing?

## Conventions and Presentation
## Editing Level 1: Conventions
# Dash for—*Emphasis!*

In the exciting world of track and field, dashes are the events where runners sprint all-out from start to finish. In the exciting world of punctuation—periods, commas, colons, semicolons—dashes are *not* about sprinting. They're about rhythm and emphasis. Writers use dashes when they want readers to pause, linger, or notice something important or surprising. Writers also use dashes in dialogue to show when the person speaking has been interrupted. Edgar Allan Poe, master of the mysterious, used dashes to give his characters a distinctive way of speaking and to give sentences what he called "spirit." All that from the little old dash! Makes you want to start using them right away—doesn't it?

## A Warm-Up

Before we tear off to insert dashes in our writing, let's make sure that you know the difference between a **dash** and a **hyphen**. Here is a sentence that contains both. Circle any hyphens and put a star by any dashes you find in this sentence.

> *Our all-star team had a party—way better than last year's—at the Big River Water Park.*

Was it easy to see the difference?

Use a **hyphen** to link two words that form one idea (like *all-star*), to create new words (like *punctuation-loving writer*), or to divide a word at the end of a line (something like this).

Use a **dash** to place emphasis on particular words, to set off a comment that interrupts the sentence, and to indicate a break in speech. Here are some examples:

- Jane—ever fearless—stretched out her hand to pet the snake.
- John had never been surprised by Jane's antics—until now.
- Jane pooh-poohed John's worries, saying, "There's nothing to—"

**Note:** A dash is twice as long as a hyphen. To make a dash on a keyboard, use *two* hyphens right in a row like this--. (Or, insert the symbol called "em dash," which looks like this:—.)

Now you are ready for dashes! Remember Edgar Allan Poe— master of the mysterious? He *loved* using the dash. Here are three short samples from Poe stories. Read each one aloud with a partner. As you read, notice how dashes affect the flow and rhythm—the voice, that is.

1. TRUE!—NERVOUS—very, very dreadfully nervous I had been and am! But why *will you* say that I am mad? The disease had sharpened my senses—not destroyed—not dulled them. Above all was the sense of hearing acute.

    "The Tell-Tale Heart"

2. Pluto—this was the cat's name—was my favorite pet and playmate. I alone fed him, and he attended me wherever I went about the house.

    "The Black Cat"

3. It is possible—indeed it is far more than probable—that he was innocent of all participation in the bloody transaction that took place.

    "The Murders in the Rue Morgue"

Now that you have warmed up with a few dashes of Edgar Allan Poe, it's time for you to practice a few dashes of your own. Here are five sentences, each one needing a dash of dashes. Read each sentence aloud two times before deciding where to place any dashes. When you are ready, use a ∧ (caret) to show where you would place each dash, and write it right above the caret, like this:

He arrived which in itself was a miracle at eight o'clock sharp.

OK—your turn. Insert dashes where you think they fit:

1. All of the history reports especially the one by Rashad were fabulous.

2. Everything we owned was destroyed in the flood clothes, furniture, photos.

3. My best friend Jolene who said she would never move away moved to another state over the summer.

4. We'll be there soon in probably thirty minutes and then we'll finish our conversation.

5. I get to leave school early today I am so excited! to drive to my uncle's farm.

## Share and Compare

Meet with a partner to compare your work. Did you place dashes in the same places? Read your sentences aloud to make sure the rhythm and emphasis sound right.

# A Dash of Spice and Spirit

Mr. Poe showed that a writer could use punctuation— including the dash—to add spirit to a piece of writing. That *spirit* is the writer's voice coming through for the reader. Here's a piece of writing that could use some spice and spirit. Read it aloud quietly. Look and listen for revision opportunities—does it need stronger details? Different words? A dash or two? Use the space between the lines to insert any revisions you think will help. (Delete anything you like.)

### Olympic Skating

One of my favorite events in the Olympics is skating, speed skating, that is. The skaters are strong with powerful legs for both speed and endurance. It is so much better than figure skating, though my sister disagrees. My sister Veronica and I were fighting about which was better. Veronica says it doesn't matter how fast you can go or how far you can go. She says she likes the music and the costumes in figure skating. I don't care about music or costumes, for that matter. I told her that speed skaters go so fast they have to wear helmets. I don't think she gets it. Speed skating has helmets. It has cool long-bladed skates and futuristic, aerodynamic suits and above all speed. What could be better?

## Share and Compare

Compare your revised writing with a partner. Take turns reading your work aloud. Did you each manage to use at least one dash? Could you hear those dashes adding spirit as your partner read aloud?

### A Writer's Questions

Choose any book you especially like. Look for a passage in which the writer has used punctuation—possibly a dash—to add "spirit" to the writing. Read the passage aloud. What do you notice as a reader? How is it possible for punctuation to add voice to writing? How important is punctuation?

## Editing Level 2: Presentation
# The Power Team

**H**otel lobbies around the world feature racks of brochures advertising attractions—restaurants, theme parks, resorts, outdoor activities, parks, historical sites—in the nearby area. Every part of every brochure—pictures, logos, bright colors, bold print—is designed to get your attention and (most important of all) your business. Brochures can't speak, so they rely on good presentation to "shout out" their message. Their designers hope that a carefully selected font or photo will get you to take the important first step—to pick up that brochure and open it to see what's inside. If you do that, maybe you'll also take Step 2, which is buying the product or service. Together, Voice and Presentation make a powerful— some might say *irresistible*—team.

## Warm-Up

Your teacher and class have gathered a collection of published materials. Look through them carefully, trying to see as many samples as time permits.

Imagine these materials are all advertising something you are interested in—for example, resort hotels in a place you'd like to visit. With a partner (or in a writing circle), select three or four that really grab your attention, for whatever reason. Open them one at a time. What do you notice on the *inside*?

Look for illustrations *and* information. List every item you find, from pictures and logos to Web site addresses, prices, and phone numbers. Make your list as complete as you can. Put a check by anything you find in more than one sample.

**What's on the inside?**

_____

_____

_____

_____

_____

_____

_____

_____

Go back through your list and star those things you think are most important in moving readers to the next level, being ready to buy!

# Pass—or Buy?

Following is the rough copy for a brochure advertising a family resort in a warm spot: think California, Hawaii, Arizona, Florida, Mexico, or North Dakota. (Just seeing if you're awake.)

Pretend you are looking for a great place to vacation—and this brochure caught your eye. You opened it to find what you see on the next page. Critique this brochure, using the list you made during the warm-up. Is the "Power Team"—Voice and Presentation—at work here? Does this brochure have what it takes to move you to buy?

# Relaxa—SUN!

**P A R A D I S E**  **F O U N D!**

## Thousands of SATISFIED customers:

*"Every one of us found something to do. We would DEFINITELY think about coming back if we won the lottery."*

*—Hadler family, City of Gold, AL.*

## CALL US!!!

# Join the
# FUN!

# Relaxa—TON!

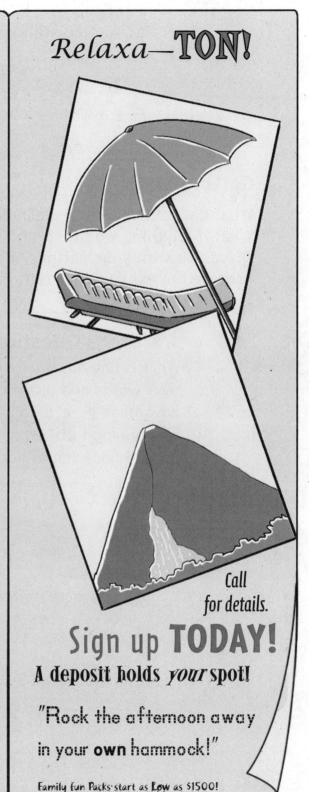

Call for details.

## Sign up TODAY!
### A deposit holds *your* spot!

*"Rock the afternoon away in your **own** hammock!"*

Family fun Packs start as **Low** as $1500!

## Decision Time—Pass or Buy?

Do the contents of this brochure have what it takes to get you to buy? Rate it on a scale of 1 to 6.

| 1 | 2 | 3 | 4 | 5 | 6 |

I'd rather
stay home

How fast
can I pack?

## Getting Specific

What does this brochure designer do well? What's missing? What if anything would you revise if you were in charge? Discuss it with your partner or in your writing circle. Be prepared to explain your critique to the class.

### A Writer's Questions

What is one advantage that a printed brochure has over words and pictures on a Web site? What is the advantage in reading a printed book over listening to a book on CD? What does the CD offer that the printed book might not?

# Presentation Matters

Suppose that your wealthy relatives own a resort in the mountains, a twenty-screen movie theater, a restaurant unlike any other on the planet, an amazing theme park with rides and attractions—or anything else your imagination can dream up. Because you are a strong writer and understand the importance of presentation, you have been given the job of helping to create the all-important inside of a two-panel brochure to advertise their business.

- Decide precisely what business you are advertising— give it a name.
- Create persuasive text to get readers to BUY.
- Plan the layout—placement of art with text and information.
- Identify key information to help anticipate and answer readers' questions.
- Create or select the perfect art—photos, illustrations, maps, graphs, etc.

**Note:** You do *not* need to be a great artist or graphic designer. If the material is copyright free, you can import art, graphics, or maps from the Internet—or borrow photos from a publication. Most graphics are copyrighted, however, so remember where you pulled the materials you plan to use and credit those sources in your work. Even easier, do a simple rough sketch, indicating what you'd like the final photo or drawing to show—making sure to place it carefully on the page. **Reminder:** Don't forget the all-important dash—use it to emphasize a key point and to add "spirit" to your text.

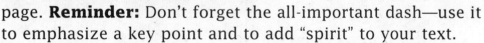

Your success will be measured by the likelihood that people will flock to the resort—or wherever. Use the next page to rough out a plan. You may also, at your teacher's discretion, create your design on the computer.

**Rough sketch . . .**

Name _____ Date _____

## Sample Paper 11

Score for Voice _____

# The Amazing Polar Bear

The amazing polar bear—also known as the sea bear or ice bear—is a threatened species. This is mainly because of humans. It is very sad. Humans hunt polars. It is dangerous to eat polar bear liver. (You might not anyway because, well, it's liver.) The liver of a polar bear has so much vitamin A that it can be toxic. Global climate change is another problem affecting the amazing polar bear. Global warming makes it hard for the amazing bears to survive.

Here are some interesting facts about the life cycle of the polar bear. Like many animals, female polar bears are very protective of their young, and not just around humans. Male polar bears have been known to kill young bears. These amazing bears don't really have natural enemies, except for humans. They don't really fear people, which can be a big problem. They live mostly in the Arctic. They hunt seals. They only use their front legs to swim! They are extremely big and they have amazingly sharp claws, but not much of a tail. Their fur and skin work together in an amazing way to help keep the polar bear warm.

Everyone should work together to keep the amazing polar bears from disappearing. A world without polar bears is a world that we definitely do not want to have as our world.

## Sources

"polar bear." Encyclopædia Britannica. 2009. Encyclopædia
    Britannica Online. 30 Oct. 2009 <http://search.eb.com/eb/
    article-9060587#986873.hook>.

## Sample Paper 12
## Score for Voice _____

# Behind the Scenes

Ask ten people, "What's your favorite movie?" and you are likely to get ten different answers. Some will start reciting lines, describing their favorite scenes, or imitating their favorite actors. But ask those same ten people, "Who is your favorite movie producer?" and you will probably get ten confused faces and a lot of silence. Most people couldn't even *name* three producers—much less pick out a favorite. A few dedicated fans know names of directors, but it takes a real movie *nut* to follow movie producers. I happen to be one of those nuts.

Here's the proof. Do you stay in your seat at the movie theater to read the credits? I do. I read all the credits at home, too—including the names of executive, associate, and assistant producers. I always wondered what all these people actually *did*, though, and since I couldn't find a single person who knew (surprise), I did a little research.

As it turns out, movie producers are responsible for just about everything connected with a film project. First, there's pressure to find a great script or an idea for a script—usually from a book. Then it has to be adapted (books are too long to film, usually). That means finding a writer who can turn a 400–page book into a 100–page script. Next goal: money. Raising money (financing) is the hardest part, especially for a producer who is not connected to a big movie studio. The producer also has to hire a director, help hire actors and a crew, create a production schedule, find scouts to locate a good site for filming, advertise and distribute the movie—just about everything but make the popcorn. Producers have to have good communication skills, and have to remain

Name _____      Date _____

cool in stressful situations. They also need a natural feel for what might make a blockbuster. Art Linson, a successful producer, says, "You have to have an instinct for who can write and for a good idea . . ."

Here's the tricky part, though. Even with the best script and greatest actors in the world, many things can (and do) go wrong. Actors have tantrums and walk off the set, equipment fails, stunt people get injured, the weather doesn't cooperate, the project runs out of money—or someone dies before they can finish. Have you ever watched a really bad movie and wondered how they ever got money to make it at all? Here's what probably happened. They started filming, the money ran out, and they had to squeak by on a really tight budget. Cutting too many corners can result in movies nobody wants to watch—even for free! And good luck getting financing after that!

Despite these problems, I hope to be a producer one day. I can handle stress (you should meet my family), and I always know which books would make good movies. Jerry Bruckheimer, producer of the *Pirates of the Caribbean* movies once said, "I only make movies I want to go see." That's my plan, too! Now, if I can just figure out the financing part . . .

### Sources

Dannenfeldt, Diane. "How Movie Producers Work." HowStuffWorks.com. 24 April 2008 <http://entertainment.howstuffworks.com/movie-producer.htm>.

Bernard Weinraub. "For a Film Producer, Success Runs Hard Into Nervousness." The New York Times. 28 Sept 1992 <http://www.nytimes.com/1992/09/28/movies/for-a-film-producer-success-runs-hard-into-nervousness.html>.

"Jerry Bruckheimer Quotes." BrainyQuote.com. BrainyMedia.com. 2009 <http://www.brainyquote.com/quotes/authors/j/jerry_bruckheimer.html>.

Name _____  Date _____

# Revising Checklist for Voice

☐ I feel strongly about this topic, so it was EASY to show that. OR . . .

☐ I plan to change my topic to _____

☐ I know a LOT about this topic, so I sound confident. OR . . .

☐ I plan to get more information from _____

☐ I read this aloud to myself, and it sounds *just like* ME.

☐ I also shared my writing with _____

That person's rating of my voice:

| 1 | 2 | 3 | 4 | 5 | 6 |
|---|---|---|---|---|---|

☐ I think a reader would *love* to share this aloud.

☐ I have highlighted any parts that need to be stronger. I plan to

  ☐ add details to make the writing more interesting.

  ☐ say what I *really* think and feel (write as if I *mean it*).

  ☐ use different words to give the writing life or energy.

☐ This is my purpose: _____

  My voice is ☐ a good fit for this purpose ☐ not quite right

☐ Here's how I want readers to feel: _____

☐ My voice will make them feel this way.

☐ I used punctuation carefully so that when someone reads this aloud, it will sound just the way I intended it to sound.

> **Note** Your voice is really YOU on the page. Are you there? Are you at home in your writing? Do you speak right *to* readers?

# Word Choice

Have you ever hunted for rocks or shells at the beach? Leaves in the forest? If so, you know that you might pick up a dozen possibilities before finding the one that looks and feels just right. You turn it over, trying to see it from all angles, holding it to the light, getting the feel of it in your hand. Collectors are choosy people. Good writers are choosy, too; they're forever seeking that perfect word that makes all the difference. That's the focus of this unit: making strong word choices.

Words create meaning, of course—but they do a lot more. *The wind hummed in the treetops* may soothe readers, while *The wind wailed eerily, snaking its way through the canyon* might give us the chills. Words create mood and imagery. They change what we see in our mind and how we feel as we read. No wonder **Word Choice** matters so much.

**In this unit, you'll work on several strategies for choosing the right words and getting rid of those you don't need. You'll learn to**

- use sensory language to create movies in a reader's mind.

- borrow words from strong writers—and make them your own.

- replace flat, colorless words with language that's vivid and precise.

- cut distracting clutter that smothers the writer's message.

## Sample Paper 13
## Score for Word Choice _____

# Pasta, Pasta, Pasta

My sister Sheri is learning to cook, and I guess that makes the rest of our family her lab rats. She's not that bad, but the thing that's hard to stomach is she's totally hung up on pasta. It seems to be the only thing we ever eat. I don't even have to ask what's on the menu. The only surprise is what shape dinner will come in—long spaghetti one night, flat wide lasagna the next, fusilli spirals the next . . . you get the idea. Guests might assume we're an Italian family with relatives in Tuscany. Actually, my great, great, great grandparents came from Ireland (and they ate fish and vegetables).

Don't get me wrong. I *like* pasta—at least I used to. My mom tells me to be patient, to let Sheri get really good at this, and then she will move on. I say she is good enough now. I mean, who ruins pasta? (Well OK, our school cafeteria could, but they have extraordinary talents.)

Here's one more thing. Sheri always imagines she is cooking for twenty-five. The pasta arrives in a huge mound. The table groans as she lowers the platter (or maybe that's my dad). We eat until we are bursting, and it doesn't even make a dent. Mom (ever cheerful) says, "Oh, good—we'll have some leftovers!" This is not what you want to hear when you're about to explode.

This whole pasta thing has to stop. I see pasta in my sleep—a platoon of linguine, ziti, rigatoni, farfalle, rotini, and conchiglie marching by and commanding me to join them. It really has gone too far. Maybe Sheri could get married. She's 17, she can cook, and . . . well, she can *really cook!* There must be a nice Italian pasta fanatic out there who could help us out. Next week is my birthday, and when I blow out my candles on my manicotti cake, I think you can guess what I will be wishing for.

## Sample Paper 14
## Score for Word Choice _____

# Autumn

Crunching through the crispy leaves, my brown eyes gaze at the wondrous bright blue of the shimmering morning sky with the fluffy, puffy clouds sailing happily across it like tiny little boats and the happy sounds of chirping birds filling the crispy air with the happy ringing of their bright, cheerful songs. The snappy, crispy air gently caresses my face with its frosty cold fingers as I stroll briskly through the many colored leaves and tender, bendable twigs surrounding the wandering, meandering path.

Fresh cool breezes softly fluff my silky hair as I look intently across the glimmering glow of the ever-changing forest with its crunchy, colorful leaves rustling softly in the chilly, vibrant wind. I deeply inhale the smoldering warmth of blazing fall fires and the simmering, steamy goodness of hearty homemade soup anxiously warming on the glowing orange-red burner of the sizzling hot stove. Autumn is my favorite time of year!

# Word Choice

**The WRITER...**
chooses words with just
the right shade of meaning.

**So the READER...**
_____
_____
_____

**So the READER...**
_____
_____
_____

**The WRITER...**
uses sensory words
and phrases.

**So the READER...**
_____
_____
_____

**The WRITER...**
uses powerful verbs.

**So the READER...**
_____
_____
_____

**The WRITER...**
keeps it concise.

# Making Movies

**W**e understand the world through our senses. As author Diane Ackerman explains, even the tiniest clues change what we see, hear, feel, smell, or taste.

The senses feed shards of information to the brain like microscopic pieces of a jigsaw puzzle. When enough "pieces" assemble, the brain says *Cow. I see a cow.* This may happen before the whole animal is visible; the sensory "drawing" of a cow may be an outline, or half an animal, or two eyes, ears, and a nose.

*A Natural History of the Senses*
by Diane Ackerman

Just a suggestion—half an outline or an ear or even a loud moo—is all it takes to put the picture of a cow in your mind. And once it's there, you might also smell the hay—or the cow manure. You might also hear the sound of cows munching or lowing, or feel the soft hair on a cow's face, its warm breath and rough tongue on your fingers. Sensory language—words and phrases that *suggest* sights, sounds, feelings, smells, and tastes —create a rich experience for readers, pulling them into the writer's world by making multi-sensory movies in their minds.

# Sharing an Example: *Town Early*

Author Barry Bauska seems to know this town well. As you read his description of a town waking up, be on the lookout for *sensory language*—words and phrases that describe or suggest sights, sounds, feelings, smells, or tastes. Read the following passage aloud quietly to get the full effect.

It is early morning. Not "farm early": up an hour before dawn to break the ice in the stock watering troughs. Not that early. Just "town early," with things coming slowly to life.

The service station owner moves among his pumps, unlocking each in sequence, setting out the metal signs: Full-Service, Self-Serve, Pull Ahead to Forward Pump. He puts out the garbage cans and the squeegees and water for windshields, then sets a small rack of oil cans precisely between two pumps. He surveys the ground in front of him, spies a handful of discarded lottery tickets and pull-tabs. He bends down to collect them, scans the numbers expertly for possible winners, then drops the tickets into the trash can...

Somewhere in the distance a lawn mower clears its throat, nearly dies in the effort, then spurts to life. A freight train intones its way past the three or four street crossings it must negotiate. There is a crashing and banging as the cars brake to a stop, roll backwards a few yards, then clump together in a final, grinding statement.

*Town Early*
by Barry Bauska

Name ......................................................... Date .........................................................

## Sensory Reaction

Close your eyes for a moment. See the scene Bauska describes. If the picture in your mind were a movie, what could you

- see? _____
  _____

- hear? _____
  _____

- feel? _____
  _____

- smell and/or taste? _____
  _____

Quickly record your impressions opposite the bulleted words. Look back at the passage, more than once. Also, keep that movie running in your mind.

## Reflection

Author Barry Bauska appeals to *almost* all of our senses in his description of a sleepy town coming to life. But—is there one sense he focuses on more than others? Write your thoughts here:

_____

Did anything set off your sense of taste? What if the author asked you to revise the passage, adding just one line that would appeal to readers' sense of taste? What might you add? Try it now. Just use a caret (∧) to show where the line would go in the passage, then write that line here:

_____
_____

# Reading on Full Alert

Here's a piece of descriptive writing about a football game suddenly interrupted by a tornado. Read it carefully, with your sensory radar on full alert. Underline any words or phrases that *describe* OR *suggest* sights, sounds, feelings, smells, or tastes.

## The Tornado

It was a cool afternoon with fog so thick you could eat it with a spoon. The tops of the wheat stalks in the neighboring field were frozen, and when the wind rattled them, it sounded like soft chimes. A perfect day for football.

Running down the field to the end zone, I could hear the huffing of hard breathing and imagine the feel of fingers on my shirt. But the quarterback had thrown a perfect pass, and no one was fast enough to catch me but myself. I wasn't about to let that happen.

Touchdown! As I crossed the goal line, I celebrated by tossing the ball into the air. My teammates gathered at the goalposts. We all pushed and squeezed to get a hand on the cold metal, and then looked up to watch the goalposts shaking. We all saw it at the same time—a dark, ominous-looking cloud formation. The wind was spinning around, molding the wispy puffs into something dreaded here in Iowa: a funnel cloud.

This was nothing out of the ordinary, so we kept playing even after the icicle-like wheat was practically being uprooted by the wind. My team had scored nearly fifty points when the wind came whistling past my ears like an out-of-tune pipe organ. My friends stopped moving. The football rolled on the grass, and everyone turned to see what they knew was coming. The tornado was on the very doorstep of our field, and we ran, the mud sucking at our feet, and thin arrows of frozen wheat stinging our arms and necks.

## De-Sensitize

Now ask yourself, "What if a writer took OUT all of that sensory detail? What would be left?" Guess what? That's exactly what you're going to do. Your teacher will provide further directions. You'll need scratch paper and a pencil.

# Your Turn to Be Sens-ational

Picture yourself in a place—any place—where your senses would be on full alert. A place with vivid, impossible-to-ignore sights, sounds, feelings, smells, or tastes. Close your eyes for a full minute and take it all in. Then, make some notes:

- I see _____
- I hear _____
- I feel _____
- I smell _____
- I taste _____

Look over your notes. Are some lines blank? That's OK. Good description shouldn't be a list of the five sensory groups. Put a star by the three or four details that REALLY stand out—your strongest impressions. Then, on your own paper, write a descriptive paragraph or poem (your choice) using those details plus any others that come into your mind as you write. Make a movie for the reader.

## Share and Compare

Meet with a partner (or in a writing circle) to share your writing. Listen carefully to each writer's words. What sort of movie does the writing make in your mind? Share your impressions with the writer.

### A Writer's Questions

Which of the five senses do writers appeal to most often? Least often? What kinds of sensory details do *you* find most appealing? How can you remember to include those details in your own writing?

### Putting It to the Test

Suppose you are taking a writing test that involves description, either as the primary focus (Describe a place so vividly that the reader will feel he or she is there.) or as one paragraph in a longer piece (for example, you might describe a memorable person, the setting for a story, or a famous invention). Almost every writer taking that same test will describe things they see. How can you make your description stand out from others?

# Reading to Write

The more words you have to choose from, the more powerful your writing will be. Where will you get new words? From conversation, of course, and sometimes from films, from working crossword puzzles, or from playing other word games. And of course, from reading. Reading builds vocabulary whether you hold the book in your hand or listen to it on a CD. What's more—not to state the obvious here— the stronger the *author's* vocabulary, the more new and wonderful words you will learn.

## Sharing an Example: *Escape! The Story of The Great Houdini*

Following is an example from the book *Escape! The Story of The Great Houdini* by Sid Fleischman. Read the passage carefully, pencil in hand, underlining words you find striking. These could be words that

- you know and like.
- just sound interesting, whether you know them or not.
- you would like to use in your own writing.

What exactly did he do that so excited the world's imagination? What razzle-dazzle fixed the name Houdini in the public memory so firmly that it is still remembered today, more than eighty years after his final disappearing act?

Watch him.

Tightly strapped and buckled into a canvas straitjacket designed to restrain the violently insane, he is being raised by his ankles to dangle like a fish from the cornice of a tall building. He wriggles free as adroitly as a moth emerges from a cocoon. The crowd cheers. Can nothing hold the great escape artist?

After recrowning himself the "King of Handcuffs," a defiant Houdini is being shackled at the wrists and ankles. He is quickly nailed inside a wooden packing case and thrown into the untidy waters of New York Harbor. Moments later, he splashes to the surface, rattling aloft the police jewelry.

He has escaped the inescapable. The skeptics are befuddled. The man must have supernatural powers!

*Escape! The Story of The Great Houdini*
by Sid Fleischman

## Share and Compare

Share your underlined words with a partner or in a writing circle. Did you underline the same words? Write your three favorites here (you do not have to agree with your partner on these choices):

1. _____

2. _____

3. _____

# What Can You Tell from Reading?

The way a word is used in a sentence can tell you a lot about it. Following are a few of our favorite words from the Fleischman passage you just read. (Maybe your favorites are on this list too—but if not, please add them at the end.) With a partner, see if you can guess if each word is a/an:

- **Noun:** name of something (person, place, object, concept)
- **Verb:** word that shows what something is or does
- **Adjective:** word that describes something
- **Adverb:** word that tells how something moves or happens

Then see if you can come up with a synonym for each word. Work for five or six minutes using your knowledge, memory, and imagination. Then check out any words that stump you, using a dictionary or thesaurus.

| Word | Part of Speech | Synonym |
|---|---|---|
| razzle-dazzle | | |
| fixed | | |
| restrain | | |
| dangle | | |
| cornice | | |
| wriggles | | |
| adroitly | | |
| emerges | | |
| defiant | | |
| shackled | | |
| untidy | | |
| aloft | | |
| skeptics | | |
| befuddled | | |
| | | |
| | | |
| | | |

## Words I Own

How well do you know the words you just explored? Let's see. With a partner, or in your writing circle, see if you can fill in the blanks of the Fleischman passage—and NO FAIR looking back! Put all notes away. Just think, remember, and picture what's happening. It is *fine* to put a synonym for the original word in the blank. Just make sure every sentence makes sense.

What exactly did he do that so excited the world's imagination? What _____ fixed the name Houdini in the public memory so firmly that it is still remembered today, more than eighty years after his final disappearing act?

Watch him.

Tightly strapped and buckled into a canvas straitjacket designed to _____ the violently insane, he is being raised by his ankles to _____ like a fish from the _____ of a tall building. He wriggles free as _____ as a moth _____ from a cocoon. The crowd cheers. Can nothing hold the great escape artist?

After recrowning himself the "King of Handcuffs," a _____ Houdini is being _____ at the wrists and ankles. He is quickly nailed inside a wooden packing case and thrown into the _____ waters of New York Harbor. Moments later, he splashes to the surface, rattling _____ the police jewelry.

He has escaped the inescapable. The skeptics are _____. The man must have supernatural powers!

Name _____ Date _____

## Check It Out

Check how well you did by following these steps:

**1.** Have one person read your filled-in copy aloud.

**2.** Have another person follow along, using the original Fleischman passage from the book.

**3.** Pause and check to see if each word matches the original—or is an acceptable synonym.

There are **14 words** on our "favorites" list. (And you may have added some we missed.) How many do you own?

- I own _____ words! I know them and will use them.
- _____ words still stump me! I need to work on these.

# Writing to Remember

Nothing builds your knowledge of words like using them in your own writing. Try that now. Imagine that you are either

- Houdini, the famous magician himself;
- one of the police officers who puts Houdini into a straitjacket or handcuffs; OR
- an observer on the street, watching Houdini escape from the straitjacket—and later from the wooden packing case tossed into the harbor.

Pick ONE of these. Then, try to "get into" your character's head. What do you see, hear, feel, and think? Use your own paper to write a short journal entry that looks at the world of Houdini from the point of view you've chosen. Try to use the three words you chose as favorites—and more from our list, too.

## Share and Compare

Share your writing with a partner or in your writing circle. Listen for favorite words that are now becoming part of your writer's vocabulary.

Name _____    Date _____

### A Writer's Question

Sid Fleischman is known for his fine use of language, and reading his work will stretch almost any writer's vocabulary. What other writers do you know whose writing you would recommend to someone who wants to expand his or her vocabulary? See if you can find one passage to share in your writing circle or with a partner.

### Putting It to the Test

Suppose you are in an on-demand writing situation, madly writing away, and the word you want just will not come to you. If a dictionary or thesaurus is not handy, what else can you do?

# Specify to Clarify

You first saw them while running to catch the bus. Now you want them—olive green convertible pants made from nylon canvas with slash pockets in the front, two back pockets with toggle closures, and two roomy cargo side pockets. And of course, they zip off at the knee! So you venture into a store. A smiling salesperson says, "May I help you?" and (here's your big moment) you answer, "I'm looking for some pants." In an effort to be helpful, the friendly salesperson brings you denims, khakis, dress slacks, rain pants, sweat pants—but not one pair of olive green convertible pants made from nylon canvas with slash pockets in the front, two back pockets with toggle closures, and two roomy cargo side pockets. Why? Because you didn't ask for them! Flat, general language rarely produces the results you're hoping for—whether you're shopping or writing.

## Sharing an Example: *Lives of the Artists*

Following is a short passage about Leonardo da Vinci, the famous sculptor, inventor, and painter. Read it aloud, quietly—pencil in hand. Underline any words and phrases you feel stand out as examples of *specific*, *lively*, or *vivid* language—words that really bring author Kathleen Krull's ideas to life.

In others, Leonardo inspired devotion. He was strong, healthy, and handsome, with a carefully brushed and curled beard. His rose-colored robes were short, unlike the long robes of most men, and he was always impeccably clean in an age when most people weren't. He couldn't even stand to have paint on his fingers.

He carried himself like royalty and had elegant manners. Usually he was calm, though he was known to blush when he was insulted (as by his arch-rival, Michelangelo). A welcome addition to parties, he devised clever riddles that made people roar with laughter, and he liked to play pranks that would make people scream—once he unleashed what appeared to be a dragon (actually a large lizard). He rode horses well, sang well, played the lyre well, and, of course, could invent his own musical instruments when necessary.

*Lives of the Artists: Masterpieces, Messes (and What the Neighbors Thought)*
by Kathleen Krull

Name _____  Date _____

## Share and Compare

Compare your underlined words and phrases with your partner's (or in a writing circle) and see whether or not you marked the same ones. Feel free to underline any examples you may have missed. Now, choose the three or four you think are the strongest and write them on this list. We filled in one example for you.

### Leonardo da Vinci: Vivid Language

1. impeccably clean _____
2. _____
3. _____
4. _____
5. _____

# Warming Up with One-Liners

With apologies to author Kathleen Krull, what if she had just written

*Leonardo da Vinci was clean, smart, and interesting.*

That general description would have made Leonardo blend in with hundreds of other people—and made Ms. Krull's writing blend in with lots of other writing, too! Anyone can write in generalities; memorable *specifics* take thought (and sometimes research).

Let's see if you can turn general, vague writing into memorable, specific writing. We'll warm up with some sentences. Read each one to get the writer's message. Then rewrite it, replacing vague, general language with specific details. **HINT:** Don't forget the importance of sensory details—and precise words!

**Example Revision**

**Before:** The dog went down the street, watching out for things.

**After:** The neighbor's black Lab, Cosmo, raced recklessly down the busy street, dodging trucks and skateboarders, yellow eyes ablaze.

**Your Turn . . .**

**Before:** We had a great time at the party and did fun stuff.

**After:** _____

_____

**Before:** The plants in the window were so nice and special.

**After:** _____

_____

**Before:** When the weather changed, we left.

**After:** _____

_____

## Share and Compare

Meet with your partner or in a writing circle to compare revisions. As each writer shares, think about the "movie" playing in your mind.

On a scale of 1 (it's a start) to 10 (get ready to faint), how strong is your *strongest revision?*

| 1 | 2 | 3 | 4 | 5 | 6 | 7 | 8 | 9 | 10 |

Share your very best revision with the whole class.

## Putting the Reader at the Scene

Think of a person you know well enough to describe vividly. It might be:

- a parent or grandparent
- another relative
- a personal friend or family friend
- a teacher
- a neighbor
- yourself

Your goal is to choose words and create phrases that will bring this person to life on paper. First, do a little prewriting by

- **rereading** the passage about Leonardo da Vinci, the one about Houdini (from the previous lesson)—or another description of a person by a favorite author of yours.
- **listing** details about the person you've chosen to describe.
- **drawing** a sketch of that person.

Use your own paper and write for 15 minutes or more. Write a description you'd like to read yourself. Create at least three moments worth underlining.

## Share and Compare

Take a moment now to read your description carefully to yourself first. Watch out for flavorless words like these:

- *nice*
- *good*
- *pretty*
- *fun*

Cross them out and add some detail, verve, life, color, spice, zest, gusto, zing, and pizzazz. When you finish, share your vivid character with your partner or writing circle.

Name _____    Date _____

### A Writer's Question

When you turn flat, dull language into vivid, lively language, you certainly improve your Word Choice. But are there any other traits that are likely to get stronger at the same time?

### Putting It to the Test

You have just finished your story or essay in an on-demand writing situation. You're tired. You need to stretch. You don't feel like reading that essay over. Should you, though? What difference will it really make? In about one minute, you can look quickly for one of the "deadlies" (vague words that readers dislike: *nice, good, great, fun, special*). And you could replace each one with something vivid, colorful, and precise. One minute and you might add a point to your score. What other quick revisions or edits could you do in one minute?

# Cut the Clutter!

**T**here's a reason STOP signs have only one word on them. STOP is the only word needed. It gets the job done, quickly and precisely. Imagine if the sign read this way: "You are approaching a street containing cars moving swiftly in either direction. Please decrease the speed of your vehicle gradually until it comes to a full and complete stop at the white line." Whew! Only fast readers would dare drive. Good word choice demands choosing the right words for the job, not tossing every word you can think of at your victim—uh, reader. In this lesson, we'll work on cutting clutter that threatens to smother the writer's big idea.

## Sharing an Example

Extra words create clutter, which the reader has to sift through to get to the main idea. Not every reader is willing to work that hard. Read the following piece to decide whether this writer got right to the point or cluttered up the message. Mark your response under **My Thoughts**.

I walked down the aisle of the airplane, between the rows of seats, and found the seat that had been assigned to me when I checked in. The plane was almost full—not totally full, but very close to being full. The travelers included men, women, older people, younger people, children, families, and people traveling alone. I hoped that whomever was assigned the seat next to my seat would be a quiet person, not someone who was interested in talking the whole way to Oakland. I like it better when I can sit next to someone who doesn't like to talk all the time instead of sitting next to someone who has to talk every single minute. If I can just read my book and listen to my music, I feel pretty happy. Reading my book and listening to my music helps me to relax and not worry about flying. I get nervous and worried when I fly, but if I read or listen to music, it helps.

(168 words)

## My Thoughts

As a reader, what are your thoughts and feelings about this piece of writing?

☐ The writer actually needs to say a little *more* about why it's good to sit near a quiet person. He doesn't fully explain it.

☐ It's a *little* wordy, but extra details help the reader get the message.

☐ Good grief. Cut the clutter! Just say it!!!!

# Revising with a Partner

Working with a partner, read the passage again. (**Hint:** Reading the passage aloud is helpful.) Together, revise the passage by following these steps:

**1.** Eliminate the clutter, crossing out any unnecessary words, phrases, and sentences.

**2.** Discuss the writer's big idea. What is the MAIN thing this writer is trying to tell readers?

**3.** Add any details that will make the piece more clear—or give it more voice.

**4.** Read your whole revision aloud and make any final changes that smooth the flow.

Be prepared to share your revision in a writing circle or with the whole class.

## Let's Compare

Compare our revised version with yours. This is only one possibility. Does our revision resemble yours?

> I walked down the aisle to my seat, weaving my way through travelers of all ages. I hoped that whomever wound up sitting next to me wouldn't want to chat all the way to Oakland. I hate flying. If I could read my book and listen to some music, I'd relax. Otherwise, I'd be a nervous wreck.
>
> (57 words)

After a close look at this version and your revised version, put a check (√) next to the sentence that best describes how they compare.

☐ We cut even more. Ours is *really* short.

☐ We cut out about the same amount.

☐ We cut fewer words but still like our paragraph.

☐ We cut fewer words—but next time we'd cut more!

## Revising on Your Own

Here's another chance for you to cut excess language that smothers the writer's main idea. Carefully read the following piece about weather. Then revise it, following the same steps you followed for the airplane piece, only this time, work on your own. See if you can cut this to 80 words max.

**Hint:** Feel free to change any punctuation or wording. Your final copy should read smoothly—and have voice.

When I woke up, I looked out the big front window that is on the front of our house. It's a good, large window that's great for looking out. Just as I had thought, it was raining. In fact, it was really raining hard. It was coming down fast, making everything soaking wet. I guess I should have been happy and not sad, because today's rain was setting some kind of a record for consecutive rainy days in a row for our area. With today's rain, we had reached a total of something like thirty-five days in a row of rain. Thirty-five days of rain is a lot of rain! The local news stations would be talking about this all day and sending reporters out into different parts of town to film the rain for their weather reports so we could watch the rain on the news. There's nothing to be all that happy about or celebrate if you ask me. This is winter. The news should be about why it hasn't snowed this winter, not about all the days it has rained and rained.

(185 words)

## Share and Compare

Share your revision with a partner. Were you able to clean up the clutter? What kinds of changes did you make?

- [ ] I cut a little.

- [ ] I cut a LOT!

- [ ] I changed some wording.

- [ ] I added voice.

## Word Choice

Name _____    Date _____

### A Writer's Questions

When you cut clutter, you make writing much shorter. So does that mean that short writing is better than longer writing? Should length be one of the traits? And by the way, how does a writer know how long a piece needs to be?

### Putting It to the Test

In most writing assessments, writers are given booklets and told how many minutes they have to write. A wordy writer could run out of space, time, or both. And once time is up, going back to cut the clutter is no longer an option. How then can a writer prevent clutter in the first place? What are some things to look out for, or some strategies for keeping the amount of writing fenced in?

## Conventions and Presentation
### Editing Level 1: Conventions
# Workhorse Words

When you think of adding words to your writer's vocabulary, you probably think of words that are unusual, precise, and impressive—words like *sagacious, auspicious, serendipity*, or—well, you fill in the blank with your own new favorite! Such words, used at just the right moment, cause readers to sit up and take notice. While good writers are constantly reaching for the best words they can think of, a host of more common, everyday words remain the workhorses of daily writing. You reach for these high frequency words almost automatically, and that means that the correct spelling of these words needs to be automatic, too. A writer who takes time to look up *serendipity* may not take the trouble to check the spelling of *which, actually, library*, or *student*. No wonder the most frequently-used words are also the most frequently-misspelled words. Learn them all, and you might reduce your spelling errors by 70 to 90 percent. You'll also have happy readers, who won't be confused, thinking you mean to say something else.

# A Warm-Up

How would you characterize yourself as a speller?

☐ I'm lucky enough to be a natural speller and hardly get *any* words wrong.

☐ I'm a good speller—partly because I look up many words.

☐ I'm a good speller, and if I don't know a word, I guess.

☐ I have trouble with spelling, but I really work at it.

☐ I have trouble with spelling, and I usually don't bother with it.

Writers can turn to many resources for help with spelling, including online dictionaries and spell-check programs (which are useful, but far from foolproof!). Many writers like to have a word-at-a-glance resource like the following list of commonly used—and commonly misspelled—words. You may find it handy to copy this list of **Workhorse Words** and include it in your writing notebook or folder. Look through the list quickly and put a small star by any words you know are problems for you. When you run across a word that challenges you, and it is NOT on this list, add it.

## Workhorse Words

about, absence, accidentally, achieve, across, afraid, again, although, altogether, always, ambulance, ancient, animal, answer, appear, applaud, appreciate, actually, around, author

beautiful, beginning, belief, believe, bought, business

capital, ceiling, carelessly, chance, caught, clever, column, coming, could, create

definite, describe, design, desert, dessert, different, disappointed

effective, either, especially, Europe, everybody, everyone, exciting, exercise, experience

family, favorite, fiercely, fight, finally, forecast, foreign, fortunately, friend, frighten

grammar

happened, happiest, heard, human

immediate, importance, important, include, instruction, interest

jealous

kitchen, knowledge, knowledgeable

laundry, learned, library, lonely

maybe, medicine

necessary, necessity, neither, nervous, no one

official, opinion, opposite

particular, patient, people, physical, position, preferred, probably

quiet, quite

realize, receive, release, relieved, remember, require, rescue, responsibility

scary, science, separate, serious, should, sight, similar, someone, special, student, succeed, surprise, sweating

therefore, though, thought, through, tomatoes, trouble, truly

uncomfortable, until, usually

vacuum, value, victory

weird, we're, where, which, whole, would, writing

yield, you're

# Practice

Following are four warm-up sentences, each of which contains one or more spelling errors. Read the sentences carefully, silently, then aloud—pencil in hand. Cross out misspelled words and, using a caret (^), insert the correct word in the space right above the one you crossed out. Refer to the list of Workhorse Words on the previous page.

1. You've probly noticed how jailous everyone is of my basketball skills.

2. I was never really interisted in foren travel until my uncle invited me to go to Europ with him.

3. It was none of my sister's bussines, but she decided to push her way into this fite I was having with my best freind.

4. Forchunatly, everone was safe after this carless driver banged into the side of our van.

I found ____ errors.

## Share and Compare

Compare your editing with a partner's. Did you each find the same misspelled words? Were they easy to spot? Does reading aloud help you find spelling errors? Are all of your "corrections" correct? Double check! (By the way, do you see any spelling errors the computer's spell-check program would not catch?)

# Editing Reality

Remember, not all of the words you use will come from an organized list. Sometimes, you'll still need to turn to the dictionary or another resource. In addition, everyday editing involves more than spelling, of course. You have to use your editor's eye to check such things as:

- Capital letters
- Missing or repeated words
- Missing or incorrect punctuation
- Faulty grammar

Here are four more sentences to edit. Your focus is still *spelling*, but be on the lookout—eyes and ears—for other errors, too. Read each sentence once silently, then again aloud, pencil in hand. Correct any errors, using the correct editor's symbol. (**Hint:** Look for spelling errors first. Then go back to look for the other types of errors listed above.)

1. If you have ever done laundery, then you know the importance of seperating cloths by color to prevent the fashion dilemma of of haveing all your clothes turn the same sad shade of gray.

2. One effective way to keep prowlers of you're property is to to have a fierce dog, preferably on a chain, barking and snarling like canine burglar alarm.

3. to prevent an epidemic, it is neccesary for everone take responsablity for personal hygiene by washing they're hands several times a day

4. I think it my little brother, the pyromaniac, who acidently caused the fire in our kichen last sunday

I found _____ spelling errors. I found _____ errors altogether.

## Share and Compare

Compare your editing with your partner's. Did you find the same spelling errors? Did you find the same number of total errors? And—this is important—do your corrections *match?* If not, who is right? Anything spell-checker might miss?

# Reflection

Take a moment to look through your writing folder. If some papers are not yet edited, so much the better. Look for words you'd like to add to the Workhorse Words list. Try to add *at least* two—but include as many as you'd like. Share your additions with a partner or your writing circle teammates—they may wish to add your words to their lists.

### A Writer's Questions
As an editor of your own writing or other people's writing, what are the *hardest things* for your eagle eyes and ears to catch? How could you work to improve on this?

# The Book Jacket Challenge

**Y**ou've heard the old expression, "You can't judge a book by its cover." As a reader, do you think that's true? Either way, book covers (also called *book jackets*) are often the reason we pick up a book in the first place. A book jacket actually has several parts, and if you're not looking at *all* of them, you're missing out on some good information:

1. The **front cover** includes the book's title and (usually) an appealing illustration of some sort.

2. The **back cover** often includes quotations from readers or short clips from reviews.

3. The **inside front panel** includes a summary that previews the book's contents and suggests who might like it.

4. The **inside back panel** often contains a short bio of the author and a list of other books he or she has written.

Good readers scan all of this information with care because it helps them choose books that match their interests and tastes. That means that book jacket copy has to be *very* well written—especially number 3 on our list, the summary, our focus for this lesson.

That **inside front panel** does two main things: (1) It summarizes the book's contents without telling so much that readers don't need to read the book, and (2) it tries to persuade readers that this is a book they do NOT want to miss! Here's the tough part. It has to accomplish all this within a *very* small space—often no more than 90 or 100 words. Now that's a challenge!

# A Warm-Up

With the guidance of your teacher or librarian, explore various book jackets. Look at different kinds of books: novels, poetry, picture books, nonfiction, and others. Pay special attention to the book summary on the inside front panel.

As you explore, make a stack of books whose jackets grab your attention in some way: cover art, title, persuasive summary, or whatever. Are there some books you think you might want to read? Jot down the titles and authors here:

_____

_____

_____

_____

# Presentation Practice

## Take the Challenge

Following is the book jacket copy for the inside front panel of a new thriller. (It's not a real book—sorry!) The title is *Mysteries of the Deep,* and the intended audience is you and other readers your age. The book is about 13-year-old fraternal twins, Mariano and Celeste (whose nickname is Seal because she is a champion swimmer). They fly to Mexico to spend a month with their aunt and uncle. There they discover that Aunt Maria and Uncle Chase are not only marine biologists, but also amateur treasure hunters who spend weekends diving for gold and other treasures. Seal very much wants to join them; Mariano is frightened of sharks and doesn't think they'll find treasure anyway. Uncle Chase explains that sharks are not usually aggressive. When they're alone, Seal teases Mariano about his fears.

Meanwhile, the book's editor has a problem: The book summary won't fit into the narrow space allowed. It's 210 words long. If she makes the font smaller, the print will be too hard to read. The text can run no more than 120 words. Read the rough text with a pencil in hand. As you read, think about what this summary + persuasive essay must do: give a quick preview of the book *and* get people your age excited enough to read it—or even buy a copy. You need to

- provide a good—but *short*—**summary** of the book's plot.
- tell enough to **get readers excited**—but don't give away so much they don't need to read the book!
- use **persuasive language** that will make this book appealing.
- keep the final copy to **no more than 120 words**.

Make cuts and edits here, then write your final copy on your own paper.

## Mysteries of the Deep

When young Mariano and Celeste (whose nickname is Seal) set out to spend a month visiting their aunt and uncle in Mexico, they have no idea what sort of adventures lie waiting for them. Mariano and Celeste picture themselves swimming, beach combing, and helping their aunt and uncle, who are marine biologists, observe and photograph local species of fish. They have no idea that before the summer is over, they will be involved in a pretty exciting adventure. As it turns out, Aunt Maria and Uncle Chase are not just marine biologists. They also spend weekends diving for gold and other treasures hidden far beneath the sea. The underwater world holds many secrets and dangers, however—everything from sharks to electric eels, plus other divers who want to get to the treasure first. Super swimmer Seal is totally in favor of the adventure, but her brother Mariano thinks it could be too dangerous. He is very frightened of sharks and also worried that he is not a good enough swimmer. Seal makes fun of his fears. You won't want to miss this exciting adventure. If you love mysteries, fascinating marine animals, and surprises, this is definitely the book for you! You won't be able to turn the pages fast enough.

### A Writer's Questions

You've just finished a very difficult task: writing a front panel summary for a book you have not actually read. (But after all, it doesn't exist!) Do you think this task would be easier if you were writing about a book you HAD read? Why? Is there a particular book for which you could write a summary right now?

# Presentation Matters

Look carefully at the book jacket summary you created for *Mysteries of the Deep*. Share it with a partner or in a writing circle and together critique your summaries using the following checklist. Put a check (√) by each thing that is true.

My summary

☐ is NO MORE than 120 words long.

☐ summarizes the main plot (hunting for treasure).

☐ tells enough about the main characters so readers will want to meet them (by reading the book).

☐ tells enough to get readers excited but not TOO much. (They will need to read the book to really find out what happens.)

☐ would get a 5 or 6 in Word Choice. (Check your rubric.)

☐ uses persuasive language that would really get readers my age to check this book out. (To check this, you must find two examples and underline them.)

☐ has *voice*—as a writer, I sound excited about this book. I wrote a summary that is actually fun to read.

☐ is good enough to compete with any of the summaries I read today.

☐ would get readers of any age to read this book.

☐ is so good that editors will be tracking me down to write more of these!

## Sample Paper 15
## Score for Word Choice _____

# Desert Creatures

Being outside on a really hot day can make humans thirsty—even a little weak. Most look for shade or retreat indoors to escape. Humans can also carry water with them, jump into a swimming pool, or drop into a convenience store for a cold drink—with extra ice. But what about desert animals? How do they survive day after day in temperatures well over 100 degrees? Like humans, they have had to adapt—and some have found ingenious ways of doing so.

To begin with, desert creatures must keep their body temperatures from getting too high or low—a process called thermoregulation, or temperature control. They look for shade, burrow underground, or if they are small enough, crawl right inside plants. Desert birds have their own way of escaping the heat—flying up to cooler air or seeking a high spot on a mountain.

Desert creatures have also adapted their schedules (something humans have not quite perfected). Some are nocturnal, meaning they are active only during the night. Others are diurnal, or active during the day. Still others are crepuscular; they hunt just before the sun comes up—and again just after it goes down.

No matter the time of day, the biggest problem desert creatures face is osmoregulation, or making sure their bodies have enough water. Some need to drink water daily, while others drink only when water is available, and some don't actually "drink" water at all. They get moisture in other ways.

Although not everyone knows this, potable water often arrives in the desert in the form of early morning fog. Desert beetles take advantage of this precious water supply, letting droplets of dew form on their bodies. Presto! A refreshing drink—delivered daily, courtesy of nature.

Over thousands of years, many animals have learned to seek out stored water from things they eat, such as cactus or even tiny seeds. The kangaroo rat, for example, rarely has to drink at all! All of the water it needs comes from digesting food. These creatures also keep cool, moist air in their underground burrows by closing off the entrances during the heat of the day.

Humans are adaptable, too, of course. We wear sunscreen, light clothing to reflect heat, and big hats to shield our faces. We invented air conditioning. We dig wells and irrigate even in arid regions to help rivers and seasonal rains supply water all year. But face it: without technology, most of us couldn't survive long in extreme conditions. Desert animals, like the kangaroo rat, have adapted equally well, and have done it all without special tools or equipment. When life hangs in the balance, desert creatures find a way to succeed.

## Sources

"Desert." *Desert Climate and Animal Life.* Thurston High School 9th Grade Science Class. 22 Oct. 2009 <http://ths.sps.lane.edu/biomes/index.html>.

Eberle, Mark E. "Natural History Fieldcourse to the Desert Southwest." *Mark Eberle Homepage.* 4 Jan. 2010. Fort Hays State University. 21 Oct. 2009 <http://www.fhsu.edu/biology/Eberle>.

"White Sands National Monument." *National Park Service.* 8 Dec. 2009. U.S. Department of the Interior. October 12, 2009. <http://www.nps.gov/whsa/index.htm>.

**Sample Paper 16**
**Score for Word Choice _____**

# Forest Fires

It may not seem like it, but wildfires that burn forests are really a part of nature and can actually do some good to the forest. After a forest burns, good things can happen to the forest and the plants and animals that live in the forest that burned. People have not always thought about forest fires in this way.

Smokey Bear was first used on a poster in 1944 to tell people to be careful with fire so that forest fires caused by people would not happen as often. Forest fires also happen when lightning hits trees or plants or grass in a forest. In the old days, forest fire fighters would try to put out the fire as fast as possible. Now, some people think that letting a fire burn but watching it carefully can be a good thing. Some trees grow better and make more leaves and seeds because of a forest fire. Some trees even need fire to make their seeds open up. When forest fires burn all the stuff on the ground, it makes room for other things to grow.

Some science people are working on ways to use goats to eat stuff that grows too fast and will catch on fire and burn fast during a forest fire.

Forest fires are one of those things that aren't all bad or all good. We need to work with nature to use fire as a good thing to help forests grow strong and be a good place for animals to live.

## Sources

<http://www.dcnr.state.pa.us/FORESTRY/ffp/history.aspx>

<http://www.panda.org/about_our_earth/about_forests/deforestation/forest_fires/>

<http://www.enviroliteracy.org/article.php/46.html>

Massachusetts Institute of Technology. "Preventing Forest Fires With Tree Power: Sensor System Runs On Electricity Generated By Trees." ScienceDaily 23 September 2008. 28 October 2009 <http://www.sciencedaily.com/releases/2008/09/080922095435.htm#at>.

Name _____    Date _____

# Revising Checklist for Word Choice

☐ I found some strong words or phrases to highlight. AND . . .

☐ I <u>underlined</u> words and phrases I need to revise.

☐ I found my OWN way to say things. I avoided tired, overused expressions.

☐ I shared my writing with _____

That person's rating of my word choice:

| 1 | 2 | 3 | 4 | 5 | 6 |
|---|---|---|---|---|---|

☐ Three verbs that really work in my writing: _____, _____, and _____.

☐ I used sensory details to help readers experience _____ sights, _____ sounds, _____ feelings, _____ smells, _____ tastes.

☐ I crossed out clutter (words I did not need).

☐ I know the meaning of *every word I used.* OR, I need to look these words up:

_____, _____, _____.

☐ I replaced ALL general words like *nice, good, great,* or *wonderful* with specific, descriptive words that show an insider's understanding of this topic.

☐ If I used any NEW words, I made sure the meaning was clear.

☐ I spelled my words correctly so readers would know which words I meant.

> **Note** The words you choose make a bridge of meaning from you to your reader. Did you take time to make the BEST choices you could? Would readers learn any new words from your writing—or is there a phrase or two that might linger in their minds?

# Sentence Fluency

Fluent writing is rhythmic and easy on the ear—like a good piece of music. While such writing might not get you up on your feet dancing, it might make you want to read aloud— to others, or even just to yourself. It's easy to read fluent writing with natural expression and voice, even on the very first try. How do writers create this musical quality in writing? First, they find ways to vary their sentences by changing up beginnings, length, and total structure. Occasional repetition that is purposeful can be effective, like the cadence of an anticipated drumbeat. Too much is tiresome, like repetitious lyrics you can hardly bear to hear one more time. Fluent writers read their work aloud, searching for the tempo, the pulse that is just right. They try to hear the writing as a reader will hear it, trusting their ears to find the right rhythm, the right pattern for the words. The result is writing that dances off the page, taking readers on an enjoyable, musical journey through the writer's thinking.

**In this unit, you'll look at some strategies for making every piece of writing you create more readable. You'll learn to**

- vary sentence length and structure to enhance fluency.

- rewrite run-on sentences to end confusion and make reading easier.

- rank writing examples based on fluency and revise non-fluent writing.

- analyze fluency to discover the "secret ingredients."

## Sample Paper 17

## Score for Sentence Fluency _____

# Seals Are Great

Seals are fascinating creatures. Seals are mammals, but they live in the water and spend a lot of time underwater. Seals are classified as Pinnipeds. Pinnipeds include all sorts of seals and sea lions. Pinnipeds are divided into two groups: the eared seals or sea lions, and the earless seals or true seals. True seals have ear holes but not ear flaps. That is why they are called earless seals. They need to come up to breathe. Seals have very smooth fur. They can move through the water very rapidly because of their fur. They are often hunted for their beautiful fur.

Seals are found in oceans all over the world. They can also live in freshwater lakes. This is unusual, though. Mother seals have one baby a year. They are called pups. Seal mothers and seal pups can get lost in the crowd when big groups of seals live together on land or ice. They find each other by sound and smell. They move smoothly in the water. They don't move smoothly on the land. They move on land by sort of flopping and wiggling. The name for this is galluphing.

Seals that live in the Arctic are usually white when they are pups. This protects them. They cannot be seen against the snow. They turn brown as they grow older.

Some seals are disappearing from the earth. They have been hunted so much that only a few of them remain. Let's hope people will try to help the seals in the future.

### Sources

Alison Hill. "Get Outside!" from *SF Gate.* 12 Oct. 2009
    <http://www.sfgate.com/getoutside/pinnipeds.html>.

"Pinnipeds." NOAA Fisheries. October, 12 2009. *Office of Protected Resources.* <http://www.nmfs.noaa.gov/pr/species/mammals/ pinnipeds/>.

Name ......................................... Date ...........................

## Sample Paper 18
## Score for Sentence Fluency _____

# Sneezing Etiquette

You know what annoys me? Sneezing. Now you're probably thinking, "How insensitive! People really can't help sneezing." That's true—up to a point. But some people actually encourage it, you know? Everyone sneezes now and then— especially if they have allergies or use too much pepper or step out into bright sunshine. These are all excusable sneezes. Here are some *less* excusable sneezes.

First is the siren blast sneeze. This comes from a person who sneezes with the force of a tornado and gives a kind of rodeo yell while doing it. Please don't tell me this cannot be helped. On the contrary, this takes practice.

Then there is the little-bit-at-a-time sneezer, the person who is too shy to just let it out on the first sneeze, and so winds up sneezing eighteen times. Let it out! This same person will keep saying, "Excuse me! Oh, excuse me again! Oh, I'm *so* sorry!" The string of endless apologies is more annoying than the sneezes.

Worst of all is the person who faces you while sneezing. Fortunately, this person usually gives a warning. They start to inhale—huff, huff, huff—so you know the sneeze is coming. It's like a volcano building. *Unfortunately*, you cannot always move away (even when warned), and when the sneeze finally erupts, Volcano Person doesn't even try to avoid your food or your face. "Here, let me give you a tissue," Volcano Person says. You really don't want to be mopped up. You want to be dry.

What we need is a guide to sneezing etiquette. It's very simple. If you must sneeze, step back, turn away, and sneeze into your elbow. Always carry a tissue, and use it—then toss it! If at all possible, give one good healthy sneeze instead of a whole series of tiny sneezes. Kill the scream. Only excuse yourself once. We can't stop sneezing, maybe, but we can do it with good manners.

# Sentence Fluency

**The WRITER...**
creates smooth, rhythmic, fluid sentences.

**So the READER...**
_____
_____
_____

**The WRITER...**
uses variety or purposeful repetition.

**So the READER...**
_____
_____
_____

**The WRITER...**
creates long and short sentences—even occasional fragments.

**So the READER...**
_____
_____
_____

**The WRITER...**
begins each sentence in a meaningful way.

**So the READER...**
_____
_____
_____

# Short, Long, and In-between

**H**ave you ever packed a bucket tightly with sand, then tipped it over to create a mountain? If you slowly pour water on top of your creation, it rolls down the sides but usually not straight down. It meanders, twists and turns, speeding up or slowing down, carving a path you cannot predict.

Strong, fluent writing follows its own path, too. Writers intermix long, flowing sentences with short, snappy ones to make the overall flow more interesting. In this lesson, you will practice varying sentence length to create an unpredictable journey for readers.

## Sharing an Example: *Notes from a Liar and Her Dog*

Check out the sentence flow in this passage by author Gennifer Choldenko. It's from a book about a girl named Ant (Antonia) and her friend Harrison. Read through the passage aloud, but softly, just to get a feel for it. Read it a second time, noticing the length of the sentences. You don't have to actually count the words. Just ask yourself as you read each sentence, "Short? Medium? Long?"

The Emersons have a funny house. On the outside it looks like a farmhouse and a big old barn, only there isn't any cropland. Just a yard with a palm tree. On the inside, it's filled with carpet pieces from Harrison's Aunt Sue's carpet store. There isn't much in the way of furniture, though, unless you count the beanbag chairs. They are everywhere. At the Emersons they either don't have something or they have it in quantity, like there's never any scissors, but Harrison and I counted eleven vegetable peelers one day.

*Notes from a Liar and Her Dog*
by Gennifer Choldenko

## My Response

As you read the passage, did you notice much difference in sentence length—and did this contribute to fluency?

☐ The sentences were almost identical in length. This was NOT a fluent piece.

☐ Most sentences were the same length—but there was enough variety to give it a *little* fluency.

☐ There was SO much variety! This was *very* fluent and easy to read!

## Take a Guess

We don't want you to get hung up counting how many words a writer uses in each sentence. Writing shouldn't be like painting by numbers. But just to help you appreciate how much variety Gennifer Choldenko puts into her sentences, make some guesses. (And NO FAIR looking back until you've recorded a number!)

Number of words in the shortest sentence: _____

Number of words in the longest sentence: _____

Number of sentences (out of seven) under ten words: _____

## Share and Compare

Compare your guesses with a partner's. Then go back and look at the Choldenko passage one more time to check your numbers. Were you surprised? Or did you know from reading?

## On the Hunt for Fluency

Pick a book by any author you feel fairly certain is a fluent writer. Choose any sort of fiction or nonfiction book (except poetry). Look for a passage (about five to seven sentences) with a LOT of variety in sentence length. Read it aloud, softly, to yourself, and be ready to share it with a partner or in a writing circle. **Tip:** Count the words in the longest sentence and the shortest sentence so you can share these numbers with your classmates—after they've made a guess.

## Keep the Focus on Fluency Flowing

Say that title ten times in a row, *as fast as you can.* Just kidding . . . Instead, read this next writing example aloud *quietly.* Ask yourself, first, how much variety your ear is picking up, and second, how this affects the fluency of the piece. Then answer the short questions at the end.

It almost never snows here. Our winters are not about snow. Our winters are all about rain. I have to carry an umbrella. I have to wear a raincoat. My backpack is always soaking wet. My snowboard resides in the closet. My grandparents live in Washington. They had snow all winter. That's how winter should be. Instead, I get rain and mud. It's no fun building a mudman.

Name _____  Date _____

On a scale of 1 (No fluency—stop the sameness!) to 10 (Highly fluent—variety makes every line sing!), how would you rate this piece?

| 1 | 2 | 3 | 4 | 5 | 6 | 7 | 8 | 9 | 10 |

Without looking back (that ruins the game), how many words would you say are in this writer's shortest sentence? Trust your ears to tell you. _____ words

How many words are in the longest sentence? _____ words

## Share and Compare

Compare your rating and your guesses with a partner's. Then go back and check out the actual numbers. Did your ears tell the truth? The ear never lies.

# Strategizing and Revising

What are the best strategies you know for making writing more fluent? List as many as you can think of. It's fine to work with a partner.

1. _____

2. _____

3. _____

4. _____

Now put your strategies to work. We have left room for revision right in the original paragraph about snow versus rain on the previous page. Use cross-outs or inserts to make any changes needed to get that passage flowing. You do NOT have to write the piece over.

# Modeling Magic

Look back at the passage from the book you identified as fluent—the one you chose to share with classmates. Using that passage as a model, write about any topic you like or choose one of the following topics:

★ My own topic: _____

_____

OR . . .

- A particularly good (or bad) morning
- Best game ever
- A vivid memory
- A friend—or an interesting stranger

As you write, try to

- use the same number of sentences as the model you're following.
- begin your sentences using the same or similar words.
- make your sentences *approximately* the same length.

## Share and Compare

Share your writing with a partner. How fluent is it? Did your writing match the fluency of the passage you chose to model?

## A Writer's Questions

Why can't there be a formula for sentence fluency—
or can there? Could you always just make your first
sentence 8 words long, the second 12, the third 4,
and so on? Could this work? And if professional
writers don't count words, how on earth do they
get so much variety in their writing?

## Putting It to the Test

Let's say you're in the middle of a writing test, and
you just happen to notice that your sentences are
ALL seven or eight words long. Do you just let it go
and hope that the reader doesn't have a very good
ear for fluency? Or is there something you can do
even halfway through to make things better—more
fluent, that is?

Name ............................................ Date ............................................

# Stopping Run-ons in Their Tracks

**Y**ou've probably heard the old story "The Gingerbread Man," in which the runaway gingerbread man challenges everyone by shouting, "Run, run, run just as fast as you can. You can't catch me—I'm the Gingerbread Man!" But have you ever heard the story about the Run-on Sentence? You know, the one in which words get together to form a sentence, and more and more keep joining the line? The sentence screams, "Pile on words just as fast as you can! You can't read me—I'm a *Run-on,* man!" Well . . . even if you haven't heard it, trust us: Run-on sentences are a menace to sentence fluency—and to readers everywhere. They pile one idea on top of another and make readers breathless. (*Pssst!* You know what happened to the Gingerbread Man, right? Run-ons might suffer a similar fate at the hands of a good editor.)

## Knowing A from B

The first step in stopping run-ons in their tracks is learning to recognize them. They generally come in one of two forms:

### Type A

Type A run-ons are *two* or *more* complete sentences joined together with no capital letters or periods to separate them:

George is my friend he is tall.

Type As are relatively easy to fix. Just add a capital letter at the beginning of the second sentence and a period (or question mark or exclamation point) at the end of the first:

George is my friend. He is tall.

**Type B**

Type B run-ons are a little tougher to spot or fix. They may be a mix of complete thoughts and partial ideas slapped together with connecting words (conjunctions): *and, then, so, but, because, and so, and then, so then.*

A Type B run-on might read like this:

We left on our trip and it was a sunny day but my brother didn't feel like going and so he stayed home with my grandmother so then the rest of us left without him but we had fun anyway.

Fixing Type Bs is a bit trickier. We have to cut out some of the connecting words or sometimes form new sentences. See if you can revise our Type B example. Write on your own. Then check with a partner.

_____

_____

_____

## Finding the Real *Dave at Night*

In the following passage from Gail Carson Levine's book *Dave at Night*, Dave is describing his first day at an orphanage. We have rewritten the passage two different ways (with apologies to Ms. Levine). One version now contains Type A run-ons and one contains Type B run-ons. The other is the author's original. Read each version aloud to see if you can tell which is which. (We're confident you can.)

**Version A**

Mr. Meltzer stopped in front of a door and opened it while holding on to me inside was a nurse's office with a scale and a cot and the nurse's desk, which had a telephone on it. The nurse said hello and smiled like there was something to smile about. She weighed me, listened to my heart, and looked in my ears when she riffled through my hair for lice, she said, "I wish I had curls like yours."

☐  This is definitely the original!

☐  This version has Type A run-ons.

☐  This version has Type B run-ons.

**Version B**

Mr. Meltzer stopped in front of a door and opened it while holding on to me because inside was a nurse's office with a scale and a cot and the nurse's desk, which had a telephone on it. So then the nurse said hello and smiled like there was something to smile about and then after that she weighed me, listened to my heart, and looked in my ears but then when she riffled through my hair for lice, she said, "I wish I had curls like yours."

☐  This is definitely the original!

☐  This version has Type A run-ons.

☐  This version has Type B run-ons.

**Version C**

Mr. Meltzer stopped in front of a door and opened it while holding on to me. Inside was a nurse's office with a scale and a cot and the nurse's desk, which had a telephone on it. The nurse said hello and smiled like there was something to smile about. She weighed me, listened to my heart, and looked in my ears. When she riffled through my hair for lice, she said, "I wish I had curls like yours."

☐ This is definitely the original!

☐ This version has Type A run-ons.

☐ This version has Type B run-ons.

How sure are you about your choices?

☐ Positive! I have a real ear for fluency!

☐ Fairly sure. I think I have a 50–50 chance of being right.

☐ Not sure *at all!* All of these versions sound *exactly* alike to me!

How would you rate the fluency of Ms. Levine's original, on a scale of 1 (This is a run-on nightmare.) to 10 (This is so easy to read, a small child could do it.)?

| 1 | 2 | 3 | 4 | 5 | 6 | 7 | 8 | 9 | 10 |

## Stop that Run-on!

Here are two chances to catch and revise run-ons. Study each piece to determine whether it's an example of Type A or Type B—or a *blend* of the two. Mark each text to make any necessary changes.

**Tip 1:** Read aloud as you work. Your ears will help you catch problems your eyes alone might miss. **Tip 2:** Revise neatly— so someone else could read your revision.

## Runaway Example 1

The sun was out for the first time in ages and my brother and I were dying to play with the new lacrosse sticks we had bought with our own money so we quickly gathered all our equipment, got on our bikes and rode down to the school but there were dozens of people there with their dogs playing Frisbee so then we tried a narrow strip of grass behind the school but then the ground was so muddy there that we just decided to go back home because we could always play lacrosse another time.

☐ Type A

☐ Type B

☐ Blend

## Runaway Example 2

It was my job to walk the neighbors' dog whenever they decided to go away for the weekend they paid me five dollars for each day I worked I had to walk their dog, Doony, twice each day I also had to make sure she had food and water if she even heard me rattling her leash, she would start to bark and jump even if she didn't hear the leash, I could make her bark just by saying the word "walk" as if it were a question Doony was a sweetheart though it was really a pretty easy way to earn money.

☐ Type A

☐ Type B

☐ Blend

## Share and Compare

Meet with a partner (or in a writing circle) to take turns
sharing your revisions. Follow these three steps:

1. Talk about which type of run-on you see and hear in each
   example. Did you agree?

2. Read your revisions aloud. Only this time . . . don't read
   your own! *Trade!*

3. See if your partner or writing circle teammate has revised
   so carefully that you can now read his or her work on the
   first try. Can you? Is it run-on free?

## A Writer's Questions

Writers sometimes write fragments on purpose.
Just for emphasis. You have seen this, haven't
you? Maybe one of your favorite writers does this
frequently. Maybe you like this stylistic way of
writing enough to imitate it. So here's the question:
Would a writer ever write a *run-on* on purpose?
Can you think of any reason for doing this? Can
you find an example in literature?

## Putting It to the Test

Run-ons present at least two problems for readers.
First, they may cause confusion by piling one
thought (or more) on top of another. Second, they
may make a chunk of text so long that the thought
is hard to follow. A mix of long and short is good—
but even with long sentences, readers expect a
break now and then! Knowing all this, do you
think it's a big deal to write even one run-on in an
on-demand essay? What are the odds, from zero to
100, that your writing *might* contain a run-on? Can
you think of a way to improve your odds? How?

# Moving Up the Fluency Ranks

One of the joys of discovering rhythmic, fluent writing is reading it aloud—some might call this "performing," almost the way you might perform song lyrics or lines from a good film script or play. Reading aloud is also a great way to *identify* fluent writing. The smooth phrasing, the perfect pacing, and the variety all add up to an easy, pleasurable experience, even the first time through. In this lesson, you'll have a chance to put your reading and listening skills to work in ranking three writing examples from most to least fluent. Then you'll use what you have learned to revise a non-fluent piece of writing.

## From First to Last

Working with a partner or in a writing circle, *take turns reading* each of the following three examples aloud. (They are all written on the same topic to make comparing easier.) You'll want to read them more than once so you have a chance to judge each example as a listener *and* as a reader. Make some personal notes in the space provided.

Example A

I'm the kind of person who likes to spend time roughing it in the woods. I'm not talking about the kind of camping a lot of people do. You know what I mean. You drive your car into one of those busy campgrounds. You pull into a paved campsite. There's a wooden picnic table. There's a metal grate over the fire pit.

You can't really call this camping. There's an outlet for electricity right next to the table. There's no hiking involved. There's only a five-foot walk from your car to the place where your tent will go. There are people everywhere. There's noise all night. You call this roughing it? I don't think so.

## My Notes

_____

_____

_____

_____

### Example B

    I love to go real camping and hiking in the woods. You get to use so many different skills for example you learn to read a map you get to build a fire, using a compass, and purifying water. Carrying a cool pocketknife is cool. And choosing the right camping spot. Watch out for wild animals is my advice! I really love all the equipment and packing and being ready for anything. But rain can be bad too, though, because if your sleeping bag gets wet, that's bad, too, or even your food. Knowing how to surviving in the wilderness is the real challenge. In the woods.

## My Notes

_____

_____

_____

_____

Example C

I love to hike and camp in the woods—but only if it's a real backpacking adventure. Don't get me wrong. I'm not an outdoor snob. It's just that driving a big *RV* (recreational vehicle) loaded down with all the comforts of home, including television and down pillows, doesn't exactly call for survival skills. You can't really say you're "camping" if all you do is drive in, connect the hook-ups, set up the lawn chairs, and grab a cold drink from the fridge. If you sleep outdoors with no *TV* or running water, and fish for your dinner, you've earned the right to say you're "roughing it."

## My Notes

_____

_____

_____

_____

_____

## Fluency Rankings

Work with your partner or your writing circle to answer the following questions. Based on your experience reading and listening, which example is

- most fluent? _____
- least fluent? _____
- somewhere in the middle? _____

What are some things the *less fluent* writers did that would call for revision?

1. _____

2. _____

3. _____

What are some things the *most fluent* writer did to make that passage flow smoothly?

**1.** _____

**2.** _____

**3.** _____

## Moving Up in the Ranks

Following is a piece that might not fare so well in the fluency ranking game. But as an experienced reviser, you can help.

Read the piece carefully and ask yourself, "How can I make this sound more fluent?" Look back at your notes—and at the example you marked as fluent.

**HINT:** Use ANY strategy you like: *cross out or add words, change wording, rewrite or combine sentences*—whatever it takes. We provided room for revision so that you do NOT need to recopy.

I was standing there in the bright, hot sun. The bright, hot sun was making me squint and I didn't want to shield my eyes because I wanted to look through my binoculars. There were birds all around some might even be bald eagles but I had to look away from the bright sun because my eyes needed a rest I wanted to see a bald eagle though so I could tell my friends that I had spotted a bald eagle, which is an endangered species. When I looked back into the binoculars, I saw some birds flying over the lake. They were flying low. Flying over the water. They could be fishing. Then I saw its white head it dropped close to the water. The bald eagle dropped down close to the water for a moment and sure enough he caught a fish I was looking at a bald eagle carrying a fish. The symbol of our country. And I was staring right at it. There. Fishing. At the lake.

## Share and Compare

Read your revised piece once aloud *quietly*—just to yourself. Listen to the rhythm and flow. Rate your fluency from 1 (Good grief! Were my ears on vacation??) to 10 (Smooth and mellow—man, you could *dance* to this!).

| 1 | 2 | 3 | 4 | 5 | 6 | 7 | 8 | 9 | 10 |

Then meet with a partner or in your writing circle to share your revised paragraphs. As in the previous lesson, trade! Try reading someone else's revision—with no rehearsal. How easy is it, on a scale of 1 (Rough going—I could NOT read this!) to 10 (Piece of cake—smooth and flowing!).

| 1 | 2 | 3 | 4 | 5 | 6 | 7 | 8 | 9 | 10 |

Talk about the kinds of changes you made. What do writers actually do when they revise for fluency?

 ## A Writer's Questions

What are your top two revision strategies when revising for fluency? Who is the most fluent writer you can think of? What are that writer's fluency secrets?

## Putting It to the Test

In a testing situation, it's sometimes difficult (or impossible because of no-talking rules) to read your writing aloud, no matter how much that might help. How can you check the fluency of your writing when reading aloud is not an option?

# Finding the Secret Ingredients

Think back to the time when you couldn't ride a bike, swim, jump rope, or make toast without burning it. Probably seems like a long time ago. Can you recall how you learned to do these things? Practice, sure. But in addition, maybe you had a chance to watch someone else, someone who knew exactly how to bike, swim, dance, cook—or whatever. Watching a good model or mentor can give you a visual sense of how something looks *as it's happening*. You can almost feel yourself doing the same thing. We can learn a lot about writing in this way, too. Unfortunately, most of us don't get to peek over the shoulder of a favorite author as he or she writes—but we can pick up a book (the final, published draft). For this lesson, you will need to do just that. Find a new or old favorite—even a book you're currently reading. Anything fluent will do.

## Sharing an Example: *The Animal Dialogues: Uncommon Encounters in the Wild*

Before looking at your own book choice, read the following short passage from a book we chose, *The Animal Dialogues* by Craig Childs. This book is filled with fluent, rhythmic sentences, linked together to form smooth, flowing paragraphs. What we want to ask you is, What is this writer's secret? What makes his writing so fluent? Listen . . . and think about it.

Pronghorn fawns spend most of their time alone, inert on the ground until they are strong enough to make a thirty-mile-per-hour sprint. It may take as little as three days to develop that kind of speed, at which point they can keep pace with mildly panicked adults. Still, they are not fast enough for a serious chase, so for eight weeks they keep to the ground. Within hours, sometimes minutes, of birth, they seek a hiding place, drop, and wait. The technique works. Wildlife researchers have observed standing fawns from a distance, but when they have walked down, startling the fawns into hiding, they have been unable to find the animals. A group of three observers walked the sagebrush for two hours without finding the fawns they had been watching. I once saw a set of photographs showing a Labrador retriever nearly stepping over a hidden fawn and never touching it.

*The Animal Dialogues: Uncommon Encounters in the Wild*
by Craig Childs

# Figuring Out the Ingredients

A really good cook can taste something fantastic and make a pretty good guess about the ingredients—without ever seeing a recipe. You're going to try something similar, only you'll be figuring out the "ingredients" for fluent writing.

1. Start by reading the Craig Childs passage aloud, softly, to yourself. How smoothly does it flow?

2. Look at the passage again, pencil in hand. Underline the first four words of each sentence. Then underline any transitional words or phrases: *at which point, still, within hours, once,* and so forth.

Name _____    Date _____

**3.** Answer some easy questions—the answers might hold clues about fluency:

- How long (about) is this writer's longest sentence? _____ words

- How long (about) is the shortest sentence? _____ words

- Do most sentences tend to be ☐ long and flowing, or ☐ short and crisp?

- Did this writer use any fragments?          YES    NO

- Did the writer use any run-ons?          YES    NO

- Is the meaning of each sentence clear?          YES    NO

- Does the writer use transitions to connect thoughts or sentences?          YES    NO

## Quick Reflection

Based on this passage, would you be interested in reading more of this book?     YES     NO

Who is the audience for this book? Check (√) as many as you think apply.

☐ People my age

☐ Younger readers

☐ Adults—or anyone interested in animals

☐ Mainly scientists

What is ONE of Craig Childs's secret ingredients for fluent writing?

_____

# Another Great Recipe

It's time to open the book you selected. Take a few minutes to find a passage that you feel is strong in sentence fluency. (It should be about eight to ten sentences long.) Read it aloud, softly, to make sure it's the one you want. Then jot down some basic information:

Book Title: _____

Author: _____

Page number(s): _____

Now look for some clues to fluency by answering these questions:

• How easy is your selection to read aloud?

☐ Very easy even on the first try.

☐ Easy enough after two or three times through.

☐ Difficult—I had to practice a LOT.

• Check (✓) each thing that is true for your author. He or she

☐ used transitional words (*however, therefore, after a while, since, because, the next day*, and so on) to connect thoughts or sentences.

☐ wrote both long and short sentences.

☐ started sentences in a variety of ways, OR

☐ used repetition for emphasis.

☐ used fragments that really worked!

☐ used run-ons in an interesting way.

☐ wrote such clear sentences, I got the message the first time through.

## In Summary . . .

Based on your analysis, did you make a good choice? What is one secret ingredient in your author's recipe for fluent writing?

_____

Name _____ Date _____

# Modeling Magic

Following is a passage that could use some revision in fluency. Look at it carefully and read it aloud, softly, to yourself. Then discuss it with a partner or in your writing circle. You don't need to revise it. Just talk about some of the things you would do if you did revise. Then watch and listen closely as your teacher revises the passage.

Fluent writing is important. It's important because most things you write not everything but a lot of things will be read by someone. That someone is your reader. You want readers to move easily through your words you also want them to make sense of your message. If your writing is fluent writing it can be read aloud with expression and voice reading aloud is the test the best way to test fluency if you read every word of everything you write aloud and keep reading until you like the sound of it your writing will be.

## Hey—What Was the Secret Ingredient?

Meet with a partner—or with your writing circle. Talk about the things your teacher did as he or she revised the previous passage for fluency. What did he or she model that YOU could imitate as you revise your own work? See how many things you can name—and list some of them here:

1. _____

2. _____

3. _____

4. _____

5. _____

6. _____

### A Writer's Questions

Maybe the favorite book your partner (or other classmates) chose was very different from the one you chose. That's OK, though—isn't it? Can fluency come in many forms? How much does a writer's fluency influence the voice of a piece?

### Putting It to the Test

As we have seen in this lesson, transitional words (*therefore, because, however, the next day, first, second, lately, in the meantime*, and so on) influence fluency—as well as organization. How could this little piece of information be valuable to you as a writer in a testing situation?

# Conventions and Presentation
## Editing Level 1: Conventions
# Editing for *the Works!*

**I**f you've ever ordered a sandwich or pizza with "the works," you know what this expression means—everything you can think of (and maybe one or two things that you didn't think of).

Good editors make sure the message comes through. That means they have to be on the alert for . . . well, *the works*. Good writers (like you) can make the editor's job easier by removing any obstacles that get in the way of the message. And face it: You might just be your own editor. Plus, as you know, anything the writer and editor fail to catch, the reader almost certainly will!

## A Warm-Up

Do you have your editor's tools ready—copyeditor symbols, clear head, sharp eyes, ears tuned-in? Good! Then with a partner (or in your writing circle) make a quick list of things editors need to look for when they're editing for the works. List all you can think of in two minutes:

- _____
- _____
- _____
- _____
- _____
- _____
- _____

- _____
- _____

Compare your list with some of the things your classmates thought of. Did you come up with something they overlooked? If so, good for you! If they came up with something you missed, add it to your list.

Next, read the following short examples carefully—once aloud, softly, and again silently, pencil in hand. These writers were not thinking about readers (or editors), which means you've got your work cut out for you. Edit for the works, finding every error you can. **Hint:** As you finish each example, read your edited version aloud to be sure it makes sense.

[ Example A ]

why do I have to make my bed I asked my mom no one will see

it while im at school conner we go threw this every day its an

expectashion and responsibility just do it she replid

[ Example B ]

summer if their is a a better time of year id Like to know what

that is i get to sleep in everyday fishing!

[ Example C ]

alligators is cool through skary at the same time  i seen them

when my family went to florida my Dad says there sort of like living

Dinosaurs

## Share and Compare

Compare your editing with a partner's. Did you make the same corrections? There were a lot of errors! If your partner found something you missed, be sure to make any needed changes. Follow carefully as your teacher edits each example.

# An Extreme Obstacle Course

Now that you're warmed up, let's take on a tougher challenge. This writer left numerous editing obstacles for you to remove. This is not for the faint of heart! But you can do it! Follow these four steps:

1. Read the example aloud just to get the main idea—and some sense of where sentences start and stop.

2. Read it again, silently, pencil in hand, and mark the sentences by adding needed capitals or punctuation.

3. Go back a third time and read it aloud, softly, editing for spelling, punctuation, and other errors.

4. Compare your editing with a partner's, line by line. (Use a ruler to make each line stand out so you can stay focused.)

raise your hand scratch your left ear. Smile. Froun. Try to

rember the lyrics of your favrite song. Hum a litle off it. Remember

the the last time you eat popcorn. Think abowt what your

smelling right now, and wether your feet itch—or feel hot or cold.

Then stop relize that you couldnt do a single one, of these things

with out your brain inside the brain is bilions cells call neurons.

Bundle together, neurons from nerves, and nervs carry electrecal-

chemical impulses from the brain or spinal card too all ports of

the body. Nerve Impulses can travel almost instantly from your

brain clear to your feet—or to such remote places as inside your

Teeth when some one tickled your foot or drills you tooth, dont

have to wait to feel it its instantaneous

## Share and Compare

Compare your editing with your partner's. Did you mark the same errors? Feel free to make any changes that you may have missed.

What if your editing is correct and makes sense but is a little different from your partner's? Could there more than one correct way to edit some parts?

### A Writer's Questions

Some writers avoid editing because they think it takes too long. (We hope you aren't one of them.) Does it? Are there any little tricks you know that can speed up the process—without making you SO SPEEDY you overlook errors?

# The Beautiful Bulleted List

Let's say a good friend is giving you directions to get to her house. She's a fast talker—and you're scrambling to write things down on a sticky note. Close your eyes for just a moment and picture this. Now . . . in your mind, do your handwritten directions look like this:

Turn left out of the school parking lot and head up on highway 41 until you come to the first stop sign, which is right by a stand of big old oak trees, and then make a left and as soon as you can, get into the right lane because you'll make a right in about two miles, so when you come to Oakvale Road, turn right and go three more blocks. You'll see my bright red house on the left, number 1482.

Or do they look more like this:

- Left on 41
- Left at stop sign
- Right lane
- Right on Oakvale
- 3 blocks to red house on left: 1482

If they look more like the second set, we think your chances of getting to your friend's house are a LOT better. Why? Bulleted lists compress information, making it easy to read and follow. (You can even check off steps as you go.)

# A Warm-Up

Your teacher may have some examples of bulleted lists for you to look at. As you look them over, think about the different ways in which such lists are used. Where in the world of print would you expect to find them?

Following are two sets of directions for tying a square knot. Imagine you need to know how to tie this knot. An Internet search has resulted in two different versions. They contain identical information; it's just *presented differently*.

You will try tying a square knot, following directions A or B. Please do not read directions A or B *yet*. Your teacher will explain just what to do.

### Version A

## Tying a Square Knot

Learning to tie a square knot, or reef knot, is simple. Start with two shoelaces. **Tip:** The laces should be untied, but left in your shoes, so you can pull on them gently. If you take them out, you'll find this task much harder!

Follow these **7 steps:**
- Put the end of one shoelace in each hand. Call the one in your **left hand A** and the one in your **right hand B**.
- Pull straight up on **B** (right hand).
- Take **A** (left hand) and cross it over **B** to form an **X** (remember, **A** over **B**).
- Wrap **A** to the right around **B** (just the way you'd begin to tie your shoe). You now have a loose knot, with **A** sticking out to the **right**, and **B** is sticking out to the **left**. (Don't pull it tight—yet!)

- Take the end of **A** (**right** side now) and cross it over **B** to form another **X** (just as in the second step).
- Wrap **A** to the left around **B**.
- Pull on the shoelace ends to tighten up your knot.

**Reminder: Left over right,** then under. **Right over left,** then under again. Pull the ends tight! When you finish, it looks something like this:

Version B

## Tying a Square Knot

Learning to tie a square knot, often referred to as a reef knot, correctly is a pretty simple task. The only thing easier, as you will discover, is untying one. You will need to start with two shoelaces. Keep them in your shoes, but untie them so they're loose. To start, put the end of one shoelace in each hand. Refer to the one in your left hand as A and the one in your right hand as B. Take A and cross it over B to form an X—remember, that's A over B. For this step, think about tying your shoes. Wrap A one time to the right around B (just the way you would begin to tie your shoe). The end of A should be pointing to the right, and the end of B should be pointing to the left. Take the end of A and cross it over B to form an X—just as you did in the second step. Wrap A once, to the left, around B. Now here comes the very last step! Pull on each of the shoelace ends to tighten up your knot. Here's a hint you may find helpful: A over B, then under. A over B, then under again. Pull the ends tight!

# Presentation Practice

## Directions of Your Own

Following directions can be tricky! Not to worry. Here's your chance to *give* the directions for a change—in the form of a bulleted list.

Choose something you know how to do well—cook a certain dish, download music to a CD, add numbers to a cell phone, score a touchdown, get from your house to a favorite spot, and so on. Your directions will need a short introduction to set up the task, then a list of steps marked with bullets. You will decide:

- Type of bullet (✌, ☺, ⇨, ✎, ★, ✐)
- Font type and size
- Special features (such as an illustration)

Try to choose a task that involves about five to eight steps—nothing too simple, nothing too complex.

## Sharing Rough Drafts

While your directions are still in rough draft form, meet with a partner. Take turns reading (and imagine yourself following) your partner's directions. If anything is unclear (perhaps a step is missing, for example), raise a question or offer a suggestion. You may also have ideas about

- an illustration that would be helpful.
- a bullet design that would be appropriate or eye catching.

## Share and Compare

Share your directions with your partner or in a writing circle. Exchange your sets of directions so you can review someone else's task. Imagine yourself following each step—do you have any concerns or questions about wording or presentation?

**A Writer's Question**

Think about ALL of the writing you do over the course of a month. Don't just think of this class. Think of all of your classes—and of any writing you do outside of school, as well. Everything from major reports to text messages counts. When might a bulleted list come in handy?

# Presentation Matters

Following is a bulleted list (surprise!) of different types of writing. Check (√) the ones for which you think a bulleted list could be helpful in presenting important information. (Think carefully before you decide—either way!)

- [ ] A birthday greeting card

- [ ] A poem about your pet

- [ ] A science report on the black-footed ferret

- [ ] A text to your dad reminding him to pick you up

- [ ] A story about a bowl of oatmeal that magically refills itself

- [ ] A birthday wish list

- [ ] A letter to your teacher explaining your week-long absence from school

- [ ] An email to your brother away at college

- [ ] A history of your hometown

- [ ] A letter to a business about a faulty product

- [ ] Reasons to vote for someone for class president

- [ ] A recipe for your favorite snack

- [ ] A brochure listing things to do if you visit Australia

- [ ] A text message to a friend

- [ ] A news clip announcing Oscar nominees for the year

- [ ] A summary of baseball players in the World Series

- [ ] A news story to be read from a teleprompter by a TV anchorperson

Name _____     Date _____

## Sample Paper 19
## Score for Sentence Fluency _____

# Movie Dinosaurs

I read a lot of books about dinosaurs and I know a lot about them from my reading. I also have an uncle who is a paleontologist, which (for anyone who might not know) is a scientist who studies fossils and ancient life forms.

The point is that dinosaurs the way they do them in the movies because first of all they are robots. You can tell by the way they move they aren't real or they are computer generated. It's kind of jerky and fake the way they move their heads and their necks and arms nothing real moves like that. You can tell when they are running after people chasing them and biting off heads and all that stuff is so ridiculous it's not at all realistic because of how they move and because dinosaurs mostly were vegetarian. Trust me this is true. You can tell this by the fossils of their teeth except for T-rex and velociraptors and a couple others they were vegetarian. You would never guess it from the movies (because how scary is it to watch a big lizard chomping on swamp grass) but dinosaurs mostly spent their time just grazing or sleeping in swamps not wasting a lot of energy chasing things they probably couldn't catch anyway. You can probably figure out it would take an enormous amount of calories to run if you were a dinosaur that weighed about fifty tons so you would not be wasting energy running after small animals that could run faster than you. The point of Hollywood is that they're just trying to get people to come to more movies by making them as scary as possible but this doesn't really work when something is fake or the same old special effects you see in every movie out there it is more annoying or maybe just boring than scary. I don't go to action movies that much anyway they're so fake it's pathetic.

**Sample Paper 20**

**Score for Sentence Fluency** _____

# Save the Black-Footed Ferret

When you hear the term "endangered species," what pops into your mind first? The bald eagle, a symbol of our country? Or maybe the blue whale, largest animal ever to live on our planet? Chances are you did not picture the black-footed ferret. This little creature may not be the rock star of the endangered list, but it is among the most threatened animals all the same.

Black-footed ferrets are not large. In fact, they are just shy of two feet long. It would take nearly 50 ferrets lined up nose to tail to equal the length of one blue whale—and getting them lined up in the first place would be an amazing feat. Ferrets cannot stand still for more than a second or two. As soon as they get together, they begin to wrestle and dance. Don't picture an organized dance like the Electric Slide. Ferrets mostly leap backwards, with their mouths open and backs arched. It's their signature move.

Despite their agility, ferrets aren't built for dancing. They're built for underground excavating in the environment where they spend most of their time—just beneath the prairie grasslands. Ferrets are slender and long, with legs and paws created for digging and hunting. Since they are nocturnal, most of their hunting is done at night; their eyes and ears are well adapted to this job. What are they hunting underground? Prairie dogs.

Black-footed ferrets eat prairie dogs almost exclusively, making them so-called "obligate carnivores," or carnivores "obligated" to eat just one thing. In years past, when prairie dogs were abundant, this worked out very well. Ferrets had plenty of food and miles of burrows. But times have changed. Humans have turned most of the prairie into farmland, housing developments, and shopping centers. These changes have eliminated both prairie dogs and their habitat.

Farmers and ranchers were not fond of what prairie dogs did to their land, so they killed them by the thousands. Unfortunately, as humans often fail to realize, killing off one species has consequences for the entire food chain. As the prairie dogs died off, the black-footed ferrets died off with them.

Now, thanks to dedicated scientists, the ferrets are being reintroduced into their natural environments in at least eight states. This is a complicated process. First, the ferrets must be raised in captivity, where they experience life in burrows partially created by people. Once they have learned to hunt and care for themselves, they can be released. This takes a long time. But scientists' efforts are paying off as wild ferret populations gradually begin to grow.

While we appreciate the efforts of these dedicated scientists, we might want to keep something else in mind. Humans have a unique power to eradicate whole populations. Restoring any population takes far more effort than protecting it in the first place. We should think about this before we decide to purposely eliminate any species from the earth.

## Sources

"Endangered Species." *World Book Kids.* from the 2010 World Book encyclopedia. October, 15 2009 <http://www.worldbookonline.com/kids/article?id=ar830695>.

"Ferret Facts." *Black-footed Ferret Recovery Program.* BFFRIT. 14 Oct. 2009 <http://www.blackfootedferret.org/ferret-facts.htm>.

Smithsonian National Zoological Park. 14 Oct. 2009. **Friends of the National Zoo.** "Recovery of Black-footed Ferrets." <http://nationalzoo.si.edu/SCBI/reproductivescience/recoverbfferret/default.cfm>.

# Revising Checklist for Sentence Fluency

☐ I read this aloud. It's smooth and easy on the ear. The writing really *flows!*

☐ I <u>underlined</u> sentence beginnings (first three to four words) to check for variety.

☐ MANY sentences begin in different ways—with words that connect ideas. OR . . .

☐ I highlighted beginnings that could use revision.

☐ Some of my sentences are long and flowing, combining several ideas. Others are short and snappy.

☐ I checked for sentence problems. As needed to revise, I:

  ☐ combined some choppy sentences to make one smooth sentence.

  ☐ got rid of run-ons.

  ☐ got rid of fragments I did not *mean* to write.

  ☐ rewrote sentences that did not sound as fluent as I wanted them to.

☐ IF I used dialogue, I read it out loud to make sure it sounded like real conversation.

☐ _____ rated my writing for Sentence Fluency:

| 1 | 2 | 3 | 4 | 5 | 6 |
|---|---|---|---|---|---|

☐ I used punctuation (and perhaps italics or ALL CAPS) to make sure readers would read my writing with *just* the right inflection.

> **Note** When it comes to checking fluency, *nothing* takes the place of reading aloud. Remember: Just because a sentence is grammatically correct, that's no sign it's fluent and beautiful. You may need to write a sentence three or four ways to discover what makes it sing. Did you do that?

# Student Rubric for Ideas

**6**
- My main message or story is clear and will hold your attention.
- I know this topic inside and out and take readers on a journey of discovery.
- I included intriguing details a reader will notice and remember.
- My writing makes a point—or focuses on a clearly defined message or issue.

**5**
- My main message or story is interesting and easy to understand.
- I share important information—and tell enough to give readers a full picture.
- My paper contains many interesting details.
- I narrowed my topic enough to give readers an in-depth look at my subject.

**4**
- A reader can identify my main idea or make sense of my story.
- I have enough information for a first draft, but more would help.
- My writing includes a few interesting details. Readers might want more.
- I think I need to narrow my topic a little. I'm trying to cover too much.

**3**
- A reader can guess what my main idea is—or tell what my story is about.
- I know enough to start—then I have to make things up.
- My details are general—things many readers already know.
- My topic feels way too BIG. I can't cover everything.

**2**
- A reader might have trouble figuring out the main message.
- The story or message isn't really clear in my mind. I just wrote to fill the page.
- I repeat things—or stop when I run out of things to say.
- I bounce from topic to topic—or list thoughts at random.

**1**
- I put my first thoughts on paper. You couldn't call it an essay or story—yet!
- I'm still figuring out my topic.

# Student Rubric for Conventions and Presentation

**6**
- A reader will have to look hard to find errors in my writing!
- I edited carefully, reading silently and aloud. This is ready to publish.
- I used conventions to bring out the meaning and voice.
- My presentation has eye appeal and makes information easy to find.

**5**
- A careful reader might find minor errors—but nothing serious.
- It *might* need a few touchups, but it's *almost* ready to publish.
- My conventions support meaning and voice.
- My presentation makes important information stand out.

**4**
- Errors are noticeable, but they won't slow readers down.
- I need to go over this one more time, reading aloud as I edit.
- My conventions support the message and make reading fairly easy.
- My presentation is OK—it draws attention to key points.

**3**
- Readers might notice the errors more than the message!
- This writing needs *a lot* of editing.
- Mistakes could puzzle readers or force them to read some things twice.
- I need to work on presentation. Readers can't tell what to focus on.

**2**
- Parts of this are not edited at all. Mistakes jump right out!
- I need to go over this line-by-line, pencil in hand, reading aloud.
- Readers will need to "edit" as they read—that should be *my* job!
- I did not think about presentation yet.

**1**
- Mistakes make this hard to read, even for me.
- I have not done any editing yet—I'm not sure how to begin.
- Even if they read it two times, I'm not sure readers will get the message.
- I need help with editing and presentation.

# Student Rubric for Organization

**6**
- Everything connects in some way to my MAIN message or story line.
- My paper is easy to follow—even with a quick reading. It has some twists and turns to make reading interesting!
- The lead is striking and will pull readers right in.
- The conclusion is original. I want to leave my readers thinking.

**5**
- I stay focused on the discussion or story all the way through.
- You can easily follow my "trail of thought."
- You'll like my lead—and it will hook you.
- My conclusion is satisfying. It wraps up the discussion or story.

**4**
- If I *did* wander, I always came back to the story or discussion.
- I think you can follow this pretty easily.
- My lead sets things up. It kicks off the story or discussion.
- My ending wraps things up.

**3**
- This isn't always easy to follow. OR
- Maybe I need *more* surprises! It might be *too* predictable.
- I have a lead—it could be more exciting.
- I have a conclusion. It's probably one you have heard before.

**2**
- I jumped from topic to topic. This is really hard to follow, even for me.
- This writing is like a messy closet! I need to move some things—or toss some out.
- I need a new lead.
- I need a new conclusion, too.

**1**
- I just wrote to get something on paper.
- Nothing goes with anything else. Don't look for a pattern!
- I didn't know how to begin.
- I didn't know how or when to stop, either.

# Student Rubric for Voice

**6**
- This is ME. You can hear my voice in every line.
- A reader would *love* sharing this aloud.
- This topic matters deeply to me. I said exactly what I felt and thought.
- I wanted to reach readers—to make them feel the way I feel.

**5**
- This voice sounds like me—it doesn't blend in with others.
- I think some readers would share this writing aloud.
- Reading this writing will convince you I care about my topic.
- This voice fits my purpose—and will get readers involved.

**4**
- I think my voice stands out from many others.
- There are some good moments to share.
- I care about this topic. I think that comes through in many parts.
- I think my voice will speak to many readers.

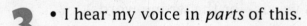

**3**
- I hear my voice in *parts* of this.
- With a little work, parts would be ready to share.
- I tried to sound excited—I couldn't do it all the time.
- This voice won't reach all readers.

**2**
- This voice blends with many others. There's barely a whisper of ME.
- I don't feel ready to share this writing—yet.
- I need a topic I know and care more about.
- I'm still figuring out my purpose and who my readers are.

**1**
- There is nothing in this writing to make it mine.
- There's no reason to share this aloud.
- I don't have any strong feelings about this topic.
- I wrote what I had to write to finish the assignment.

# Student Rubric for Word Choice

**6**
- You'll want to highlight memorable words and phrases.
- Lively verbs give my writing energy.
- Sensory details put readers right at the scene.
- You won't find clutter. Every word counts!

**5**
- My words are clear. I found *my own way* to say things.
- I used many strong verbs.
- I used sensory details in the right spots.
- There's little or no clutter.

**4**
- My words are used correctly.
- I used *some* strong verbs—and some adjectives.
- I used some sensory details—if they fit.
- Sometimes I repeated things or used words I didn't need.

**3**
- I used too many general words—or the wrong words.
- I need more verbs—or fewer modifiers!
- I need more sensory details. (Or I used TOO many!)
- It's wordy, repetitious, or overwritten.

**2**
- I used the first words I thought of.
- Most of my verbs are *is, are, was, were.* No real action!
- I told about things you *see*—but no *sounds, smells, feelings,* or *tastes.*
- It's wordy—or else I did not say enough.

**1**
- It was hard to find the right words. I did not know what to write.
- I wasn't sure how to use verbs.
- My writing doesn't help you picture things.
- I need more words—or different words.

# Student Rubric for Sentence Fluency

**6**
- My writing is smooth and easy to read on the first try.
- Sentences differ in length and begin in ways that show how ideas connect.
- You can read this expressively to bring out every ounce of voice.
- If I used dialogue, it's so real you can perform it like a play.

**5**
- My writing flows smoothly. No bumps or sudden stops!
- Sentences differ in length and structure.
- It's easy to make this paper sound fluent and smooth.
- If I used dialogue, it sounds like real conversation.

**4**
- My writing is easy to read with a little practice.
- There's enough variety to make sentences interesting.
- With a little effort, you can make this writing sound fairly fluent.
- If I used dialogue, it's pretty realistic.

**3**
- Some parts are smooth—others are choppy or rambling.
- Too many sentences start the same way or are the same length.
- To read this smoothly, you need to rehearse—and pay attention.
- If I used dialogue, it needs work.

**2**
- Choppy sentences, run-ons, or other problems make reading slow.
- I use the same sentence patterns over and over. I might have fragments I didn't want.
- To read this aloud, prepare to "smooth over" some bumpy spots.
- I didn't use dialogue. Or else I couldn't make it sound real.

**1**
- This is hard to read. I'm not sure all my "sentences" are really sentences.
- It's hard to tell where my sentences begin and end.
- Words or punctuation could be missing. Readers need to fill these in.
- I didn't try to write dialogue.